Smart Boundaries

Safe Children – A Parent's Handbook

by
Well-Being Publishing

To You,

Thank you!

Table of Contents

Introduction

Welcome to a journey where we embark on the important mission of nurturing knowledgeable, confident, and safe children. In an ever-changing world, it is essential that our little ones know about personal safety, how to spot concerning behavior, and understand the significance of consent and setting their own body boundaries. This book is crafted with the loving hands of parents, educators, and caregivers in mind, aiming to equip you with the tools and knowledge to safeguard the brightest of futures for our kids.

Imagine a world where children walk through life with the self-assurance to express their feelings, the courage to set boundaries, and the wisdom to navigate the complexities of human interaction. That's the world we aspire to cultivate through the pages of this book. We'll dive into the fundamental principles of creating an environment where conversations about safety and respect are as natural as chatting about the school day or favorite books. By fostering open, age-appropriate dialogue, we set the stage for our children to face the world with an empowered and informed perspective.

Each chapter ahead serves as a building block, reinforcing the understanding and importance of personal safety from the playroom to cyberspace. As we explore these essential topics, you'll find that the power lies in the simplicity of our message and the strength of our collective commitment to child safety. Together, let's mold a generation of children who are not only well-protected but are also advocates for their own well-being and that of their peers.

Chapter 1:
Understanding Personal Boundaries

Just as a garden has its fence, each of us has invisible lines that help us feel safe and respected - they're called personal boundaries. These boundaries are as unique as the patterns on a butterfly's wings, varying from one person to another. Understanding and honoring personal boundaries is like learning the steps to a delicate dance. It gives children the confidence to whirl through life knowing they have control over their own space, thoughts, and feelings, and that they can recognize and respect those same boundaries in others. We'll explore the basics here, laying the foundation for empowering kids to confidently say "this is my space" and "you're welcome here," creating a wonderful balance of independence and empathy.

Section 1.1: The Basics of Boundaries

Pioneering into the world of personal boundaries, we dive into the importance of understanding what they are and why they matter so much. Boundaries are the limits we set for ourselves and others, informing how we expect to be treated, what we're comfortable with, and what we're not. They are our invisible lines, marking the space where respect and safety begin.

Think of boundaries like the rules of a game; they provide a structure that helps everyone understand how to play fairly and what constitutes a foul. When everyone knows the rules, we can all enjoy the game more, feeling safe and respected. Similarly, when we understand boundaries, we build better relationships with those around us—friends, family, and even people we've just met.

Now, when we talk about personal boundaries, we're not just discussing physical space—although that's an important part. Personal boundaries also include our feelings, thoughts, and needs. It's like having our own special bubble that encases all the things that make us uniquely 'us', and it's crucial that we learn both how to protect that bubble and respect others' bubbles as well.

First things first, teach children that their bodies belong to them, and them alone. This is a primary boundary every child should know. It's essential for their self-esteem and for navigating interactions with others. By understanding this, they learn to respect their own bodies and to expect that respect in return from others.

Children should also grasp that they have the right to their own emotions and opinions. Their feelings are valid and important, even if they might be different from others'. This gives them the courage to voice their thoughts and feelings, and to stand up for themselves when needed.

Furthermore, let's talk about privacy. Privacy is a boundary that helps kids know it's okay to have their own space and time alone, whether to think, to play, or just to have a moment's peace. It teaches them the importance of having time to recharge and the recognition that everyone sometimes needs a break from the busy world around them.

Respect is the cornerstone of understanding and upholding boundaries. Kids learn respect not just through words but through actions. When they see adults respecting their boundaries, they learn that this is how everyone should be treated, and in turn, they learn to treat others the same way.

Now, boundaries can't be set in stone. They're more like guidelines that may shift and change as children grow and their comfort levels change. It's a dynamic process that requires patience and continuous learning. A boundary that feels right today might need adjustment tomorrow, and that's perfectly okay.

One of the best ways to help children understand their boundaries is through everyday examples. Discuss scenarios they might encounter, such as a classmate borrowing their pencil without asking or someone wanting to share a secret with them. Exploring these simple situations can pave the way for conversations about more complex boundaries later on.

It's never too early or too late to start discussing boundaries with kids. Even very young children can grasp the concept of "mine" and "yours," and that's a basic building block of boundary-setting. With age, the conversations can deepen and expand to include more abstract ideas, like emotional and intellectual boundaries.

Encouraging children to express when they feel a boundary has been crossed is also vital. Help them find the words to say "I'm not okay with that" or "I need space" in a safe and supportive environment. With practice, they'll gain the confidence to assert their boundaries in any situation.

Boundaries are also about saying yes to what feels good and no to what doesn't. Teaching kids to tune into their intuition and to trust their gut feelings helps them make decisions that honor their boundaries. It is a foundational aspect of building self-awareness and the ability to navigate the world with confidence.

As you can see, boundaries are a complex but foundational element of personal safety and respect. They help children understand who they are, what they value, and how they wish to interact with the world. By mastering the basics of boundaries, our kids can build healthier, happier relationships and a stronger sense of self.

So, as we journey through the rest of this chapter, we'll explore practical ways to teach and reinforce these ideas, ensuring that your child has the tools they need to stand firm in their boundaries. We will delve deeper into personal space, the power of saying no, and respecting both their own and others' limitations. It's all part of growing up safe, savvy, and secure in an ever-changing world.

Remember, every child is unique, and so are their boundaries. Our role as parents, caregivers, and educators is to guide them in discovering and setting these personal limits. By fostering an environment of understanding and respect, we enable our children to establish the foundations of a life where they feel in control, respected, and safe.

Section 1.2: Teaching Your Child About Personal Space

As we usher in an understanding of boundaries, it's crucial to enrich this journey by introducing our little ones to the notion of personal space. This invisible bubble that surrounds us serves as our intimate zone of comfort and safety. Just as a bird cherishes its nest, children ought to recognize and value their own personal space – and that of others.

Let's ignite this discussion with a fun activity. Ask your child to extend their arms out wide – that's approximately the size of their personal space. It's a space meant just for them, a boundary that others should respect. This simple visualization helps anchor the concept in a way they can physically comprehend. Remember, for kids, learning through play cements ideas more firmly than abstract talk ever could.

Delving deeper, we spotlight the scenarios where personal space is important. From standing in line at school to sitting beside someone during storytime, these everyday situations provide perfect teaching moments. Encourage your child to notice how close is too close by using simple cues. If someone can reach out and touch them without moving much, they're probably within their personal bubble. And, oh, isn't it empowering when they start nudging at that imaginary sphere, advocating for their own comfortable distance?

But don't forget, respecting personal space is a two-way street. Encourage empathy by asking your child how they feel when someone invades their bubble. Then, flip the narrative: "How do you think your friend feels when you're hugging them a bit too tightly?" Empathy is the first step to respecting others' boundaries as much as their own.

Now, what happens when a child encounters someone—adult or peer—who doesn't honor personal space? It's a tough situation. Instill in them the confidence to politely express their discomfort; equip them with phrases like, "I need a little more space, please," or "Can you step back a bit?" These are tools of empowerment, giving them a voice to protect their own zone of comfort.

Remember to celebrate their efforts. Each time they express their need for personal space or respect someone else's, acknowledge it. This positive reinforcement emboldens them to continue asserting their boundaries and respecting those of others. Validation is key in helping children understand their feelings and actions matter.

We must be role models too. Show your child how you respect the personal space of family members or strangers. Lead by example. When you give someone space, narrate your actions: "I'm stepping back to give Ms. Thompson some room because that's the kind way to interact." These lived examples become etched in their minds, shaping their daily interactions.

However, there are times when personal space might need to be breached for safety or health reasons. It's vital that children understand these exceptional situations. From a doctor's check-up to a quick safety-check by a parent before a bike ride—these are moments when our bubble might shrink temporarily, but with good reason.

It's a balancing act, teaching privacy without fostering fear. Remind your child that most people respect personal space and those who don't can often be reminded with a simple request. But should they ever feel unsafe, they must know who the trusted adults are that they can turn to. This speaks to the importance of cultivating an environment where children feel listened to and protected.

And as our children grow, their understanding of personal space will evolve. What feels okay at seven might change at ten. It's an ongoing dialogue, one that adjusts with their advancing maturity and experiences. They'll learn, for example, that cultural norms influence concepts of space, and what's acceptable among friends may differ in other relationships.

Children with sensory processing differences may have unique needs regarding personal space. Acknowledge and validate those needs by working together to establish comfortable boundaries that they can communicate to others. Custom-fit solutions foster inclusion and understanding in every social fabric our children may weave through.

Facilitating activities that differentiate "public" and "private" reinforces understanding of personal space in a broader context. This is where prompts like "Is this a public or a private place?" come in handy, guiding them to consider the appropriateness of various interactions within the invisible boundaries society sets.

Don't be daunted if the concept takes time to stick. Reiteration is the cornerstone of learning. Adopt creative ways to remind your child about personal space without chiding. Puzzles, stories, and games can all be subtly tailored to reinforce this essential life skill. Patience is your ally as your child navigates these foundational waters.

Lastly, engage with your child's caregivers and teachers. Consistency is the backbone of comprehension. When all adults in a child's life are on the same page about personal space, the child receives a coherent message, cementing the concept. Collaborate on strategies and perspectives to heighten the learning experience, making the understanding of personal space not just a lesson but a lived experience for your child.

Teaching your child about personal space is not an overnight feat. It's a journey that meanders through the years of childhood, branching out into deeper themes such as consent and bodily autonomy. In fostering this awareness, you'll find the seeds of respect, safety, and dignity that will bloom throughout their lives.

Chapter 2:
Communication Is Key

Now that we've embraced the importance of personal boundaries, let's dive into the heart of connection—communication. Picture this: a bridge being built, plank by plank, with every heart-to-heart you share with your child. Words softly spoken, ears keenly listening, and feelings expressed freely—the flow of open communication kindles trust, cultivates understanding, and creates a safety net woven with the threads of sincere dialogue. It's through this exchange that children learn their voices matter, their thoughts are valued, and their concerns are always worthy of attention. In this chapter, we're not spilling secrets or crafting complex codes. Instead, we're gently unfolding the map of effective conversation, pointing out the landmarks of clear expression, and marking the checkpoints where listening is just as vital as speaking. Remember, even when the waters seem calm, keep building that bridge, because a strong foundation in communication ensures your kids can always reach you, no matter what tides may come their way.

Section 2.1: Using Age-Appropriate Language

As we venture further into this essential conversation about personal safety, recognizing grooming, and understanding consent and body boundaries, let's pause for a moment to anchor ourselves in the delicate art of communication. We're now entering a pivotal juncture: How can we speak to our precious bits of stardust about such weighty matters in a way that's both comprehensible and sensitive to their tender age? Here lies the crux of where we aim to turn befuddling concepts into digestible morsels of knowledge.

When it comes to toddlers and preschoolers, we're scaffolding their understanding with the simplest building blocks of safety. Imagine breaking down the concept of personal boundaries into a game of "who's in my bubble?" It's an approach that feels playful yet imparts the foundational idea that they have an invisible space that's entirely their own, and others need to respect that space.

Moving into the arena of early childhood—the five to seven-year-old range—our discussions can evolve. This is an age where curiosity blossoms and so does the capacity for absorbing more complex ideas. It's here we might introduce terms like "privacy" and differentiate between "safe touches" and "unsafe touches." Be clear, using illustrations or stories to solidify these critical points, but still, keep the language soft, accessible, and, most importantly, non-threatening.

As our audience grows into the 'big-kid' stage, those aged eight to twelve, their worlds expand rapidly. They're balancing on the cusp of adolescence, making it a prime time to layer in more nuanced language. Discussions can touch on consent with phrases like "mutual respect" and "agreement," and the concept of grooming can be explained by talking about trust and gut feelings.

But how do we do this without causing alarm? We opt for a tone of empowerment. Every conversation is a brick in the fortress of their self-worth. Teach them that their feelings and comfort matter and that they have the power to express when something doesn't feel right. Use allegories or scenarios that resonate—perhaps likening personal boundaries to the rules of a sport or the natural borders of a garden.

In threading these conversations throughout their lives, keep a keen eye on your child's cues. Their questions, their expressions, their body language—all of these will guide you toward what's necessary to expand upon or simplify. Listen earnestly to their thoughts, and affirm their inquiries with respect. This ensures that they feel heard, valued, and more inclined to open up in return.

Being consistent is also key. While avoiding redundancy, reinforce these lessons in everyday interactions. For instance, discuss consent when they're playing with others: "Is it okay if you borrow her toy? Did you ask first?" Such practice embeds the concept into daily life, making it a natural part of their relational toolkit.

Avoid euphemisms that obscure the truth. While "stranger danger" is an age-old adage, it neither captures the nuance of personal safety nor does it account for the fact that, often, harm can come from familiar faces. Shoot straight, but always tailor your language to the garden they can safely play in, according to their stage of growth.

Children's books and educational shows, which are companions in the journey of raising young ones, also serve as gentle vehicles for these messages. Opt for literature and media that underline themes of body autonomy and respect—tools that reinforce what you're already nurturing at home.

When it comes to discussing boundaries and safety, split these life-lessons into episodic teachings rather than a one-time dissertation. Imagine it as the recurrence of their favorite jingle—an unfolding story where each verse unpacks a little more of the melody.

Furthermore, never underestimate the potency of praise. When children respect their own or others' boundaries, acknowledge this behavior. A "You did a great job telling Johnny you wanted to stop wrestling" rewards their action and encourages ongoing respect for personal space.

Incorporate correct anatomical terms, too. While pet names for body parts may seem less intimidating, clarity provides protection. It's important they can communicate effectively about their bodies, especially if something inappropriate occurs. Keep these explanations matter-of-fact, stripping them of any inadvertent shame or embarrassment.

For truly age-appropriate communication, reflect the diversity of families and experiences. Speak in inclusivity, recognizing that each child and family dynamic is unique. Honor these differences in the tapestry of conversations, creating a universal dialogue that speaks to all.

At the end of the day, it's not only about the words themselves; it's about the connection they create. You're weaving a web of trust—that your child will feel safe coming to you, equipped with the language they need to express themselves. This web is resilient, vibrant, and woven through the threads of love, understanding, and patience.

So let's navigate these waters with a spirit of adventure, empathy, and a continual commitment to educate. Assembling the bridge of communication with age-appropriate language is an art—uniting the wisdom of a caregiver with the learning spirit of a child. Together, we're building a vocabulary that roots itself deeply in respect, nurturing a future where personal safety and understanding flourish hand in hand.

Section 2.2: Creating an Open Dialogue

In the journey of nurturing a child's understanding of personal safety and boundaries, setting the foundation for open dialogue is perhaps one of the most vital steps. It's akin to planting a tree; you want the roots to be deep and strong, anchored in trust and comfort, so that as it grows, it weathers all sorts of storms. This section will guide you on how to cultivate that comforting space where communication blossoms.

To start, let's think about the seed of trust. Children are more likely to open up when they feel safe and trust that their feelings and words matter. As caregivers, we can build trust by being attentive listeners. Quite simply, when your child speaks, pause and give them your full attention. It shows that their voice is valuable and their experiences are worthy of notice.

But how do we ensure that this trust continues to grow? Consistency is key. Like watering a plant regularly, check in with your child often. Make conversations about their day, their feelings, and their interactions a normal part of daily life. It doesn't always have to be a sit-down chat; these talks can happen during a car ride, mealtime, or bed-time storytelling.

Sometimes, the right environment makes all the difference. Creating a cozy corner or a special 'talk time' place can make these conversations easier. It's like saying, "Here, this is our safe space where anything you say is respected and kept confidential." It sets the scene for openness and sincerity.

One might wonder though, what about those hard-to-ask questions? That's where your approach comes in. Instead of pointed queries, opt for open-ended questions. Ask about their feelings and thoughts without steering them toward what you expect to hear. Encourage them by saying things like "Tell me more about that" or "How did that make you feel?"

Patience, just like sunlight to a plant, is essential for growth. Sometimes children need time to process their thoughts or muster the courage to share something. They might circle around the topic or talk about something else first. Be patient and let them navigate the conversation at their own pace.

Now, it's important to acknowledge the big emotions. When conversations get heavy, staying calm is crucial. The way you react to tough topics will either fortify or weaken that trust. Show empathy and understanding, and resist the urge to immediately fix the problem. Instead, validate their feelings and work together to find solutions.

Of course, the dialogue isn't just about words. Nonverbal cues matter just as much. Your body language, facial expressions, and even tone of voice convey your true reaction. Ensure you're open and inviting; this will encourage your child to continue sharing.

What if your child isn't ready to talk when you are? Respect that. Let them know they can come to you anytime, that the door is always open, and then give them space. It's like letting the soil rest; sometimes that's what's needed for healthiest growth.

Let's not forget, dialogue is two-sided. Share your own experiences and feelings on an appropriate level. Children learn by example, so when they see you expressing yourself respectfully and openly, they're more inclined to do the same. It might be about how you managed a tricky situation or something new you've learned.

Now, for a crucial part of the conversation: boundaries. These can be tricky waters to navigate, but remember, setting boundaries is a sign of a healthy relationship. Explain that certain topics or words are private but do so without attaching shame to them. It's about respect, not fear.

Encouraging questions is another way to foster openness. When a child asks a question, no matter how awkward, take it seriously. This is their way of reaching out and understanding the world. Provide clear, honest answers that are age-appropriate, and don't be afraid to say you'll find out together if you don't know.

In situations when the subject matter is delicate, such as discussing abuse or inappropriate touch, anchor the conversation in safety and love. Instead of instilling fear, emphasize how you're always there to help and protect them. Remind them that they have the right to feel secure and cared for.

Remember, these conversations aren't one-time events but should be ongoing. Life is full of changes and so are the lives of children. As they grow, their understanding deepens and their curiosity grows. Keep the lines of communication adapting to their developmental stage.

Last but certainly not least, celebrate the successes. When your child comes to you with something difficult, recognize their bravery. Whether it's with words of affirmation, a hug, or a little celebratory activity, acknowledge that it's a big deal to trust someone with tough stuff.

Creating an open dialogue with your child is an ongoing journey, a mixture of art and science, empathy and strategy. It's arming them with confidence to voice their thoughts and fears, and ensuring they know that their feelings are always heard and valued. By fostering this environment, you're not only protecting them but empowering them to navigate the complexities of relationships and personal safety with confidence.

Section 2.3: Role-Playing Scenarios

Imagine playing pretend with a purpose, where you can practice what you might say or do in real-life situations that involve your personal safety and boundaries. That's precisely what role-playing scenarios are all about. They're not just games—they're valuable tools that help children understand and navigate the complexities of personal interactions in a safe and controlled environment.

Start with a simple scene. You might be at a park, and someone you don't know asks if you need help looking for your lost ball. What do you do? This scenario allows kids to think through their responses and encourages them to act out saying "no" and seeking a trusted adult.

Role-playing doesn't require any special equipment, just your imagination and sometimes a few prompts to get started. A scenario could be as straightforward as someone offering a ride home from school or as complicated as being pressured by a friend to keep a secret from parents. Guiding children through these conversations can empower them to make smart choices in real situations.

It's important for kids to understand that they have the right to say "no," even to adults or friends, if they feel uncomfortable. Practicing this through role-play can build the confidence needed to assert their boundaries. How about rehearsing what to do if someone tries to touch them in a way that doesn't feel right? By acting it out, they can learn to firmly state their discomfort and move away from the person.

In role-plays, children can also learn how to trust their instincts. If something doesn't feel quite right, it's OK to act on that feeling. Encourage them by saying, "Trust your tummy feelings. If something feels weird, it's alright to walk away."

Online interactions are just as critical. Set up a pretend game where someone they don't know messages them online. What should they do? Should they respond, tell an adult, or block the person? By simulating this scenario, children can practice the safest course of action without being in actual danger.

You can also use role-play to teach about secrets. Explain that good secrets, like surprise parties, can be fun, but bad secrets that make them uneasy should be shared with a trusted adult. Play out scenarios where someone asks them to keep an uncomfortable secret, so they get used to the idea of speaking up.

Don't forget to switch roles. Let your child play the adult sometimes, so they can see situations from different perspectives. It can be quite an eye-opener and a unique chance for them to guide the outcomes. They'll likely come up with insightful ideas on handling tricky interactions.

Role-playing can be integrated into daily routines. For instance, while heading out to a store, you can discuss and act out what to do if they can't find you suddenly. It's not about creating fear; it's about preparing them and giving them the confidence to handle themselves with poise.

It's also critical to praise children for making smart decisions during these pretend interactions. Positive reinforcement goes a long way in cementing the right behaviors. Encourage them by acknowledging the strength it takes to stand up for themselves.

Another beneficial scenario is discussing what consent looks like in play. Maybe another kid wants to borrow their toy. Role-play how to say yes or no, and respect another person's no, too. This simple act reinforces consent and respect in social play.

While discussing harder topics like inappropriate touching, it's essential to keep the role-play appropriate for their age. Simplicity is key. Phrasing like, "What if someone wants to give you a hug and you don't want to?" helps approach the subject gently.

Consider role-playing in groups with other children and parents. It can reflect real peer interactions and provide different insights. Plus, it shows that all children face similar situations and that they're not alone in learning to deal with them.

Remember to debrief after each role-play session. Ask open-ended questions about how they felt and what they might do differently next time. These conversations can deepen their understanding and allow for coaching on nuanced issues that role-playing might bring up.

Finally, let's anchor these scenarios in everyday practice. Children learn by doing, so the more they role-play, the better they'll handle themselves when faced with a challenge. Encourage them to think about their role-playing experiences when they encounter similar situations in the real world.

With role-playing scenarios, we're not just playing pretend; we're building the foundations for strong, confident, and safe children. Through thoughtful practice and lively imagination, we're equipping them with the skills to protect themselves and to assert their personal safety and boundaries with assurance.

Chapter 3:
Recognizing Grooming Behaviors

As we've learned about personal boundaries and the importance of clear, open communication, it's essential to apply that understanding to recognize when something isn't quite right. Grooming behaviors can be sneaky and confusing, but knowing what to look out for is a superpower in keeping our superheroes—our kids—safe. It's all about being a detective in spotting those sneaky moves that someone might use to gain a child's trust a little too quickly or in ways that just feel off. We're talking about special attention that crosses the comfort line, gifts with strings attached, or secrets that shouldn't be kept. Recognizing grooming isn't about being suspicious of everyone; it's about being smart, savvy, and secure when interactions with adults or even older kids don't match up with the safe, respectful boundaries we cherish. So let's turn our insights into action and empower our little ones to recognize, resist, and report behaviors that aren't up to snuff, ensuring their world remains a place where trust and safety thrive hand in hand.

Section 3.1: Grooming Tactics Explained

Grooming can be a challenging subject to approach, but understanding its dynamics is a critical step in protecting our children. As we transition from open dialogue in our previous sections, let's dive into the cunning world of grooming tactics. Grooming is a process used by offenders to build a relationship, trust, and emotional connection with a child or young person so they can manipulate, exploit and abuse them.

At the core is the 'groomer's' effort to become a special part of the child's life by filling a need, often posing as a wonderful friend who is attentive and caring. This emotional investment is the foundation upon which other dangerous behaviors may be introduced. Children crave affection and attention, and groomers exploit this need.

Grooming often begins with simple acts of kindness. The groomer might give gifts or special treats, and these may not seem out of the ordinary at first. Over time, however, these gifts can become more elaborate as the groomer's influence embeds deeper, testing boundaries and gauging the child's response.

Communication with the child often escalates to frequent check-ins, messages, or chats. The groomer may ask seemingly innocent questions about the child's life, gradually but purposefully isolating them from other friends and family members. This creates a secret world in which the groomer's influence can grow unimpeded.

Groomers can be very clever in building trust not just with the child but also with the child's family or community. They may involve themselves with the parent's activities, volunteering to assist with childcare or transportation, cementing their role as a 'trusted' adult.

The next stage could involve breaking down the child's understanding of appropriate behaviors. Groomers may share content not suitable for children, like pictures, videos, or jokes, normalizing inappropriate subjects and desensitizing the child to sexual content.

Subtly, groomers might start violating the child's physical boundaries with accidental touches or hugs that linger too long, and in this process, testing the child's reaction and degree of compliance. They might also encourage the child to keep these interactions a secret, thus creating an atmosphere of complicity.

Another tactic is to test and push the child's limits by presenting risky behaviors as exciting, normal, or a way to prove their maturity or loyalty. This may be combined with the threat or use of guilt, suggesting that not engaging in these behaviors could disappoint the groomer or harm their relationship.

In an unsettling shift, the relationship may take on an increasingly exclusive or possessive nature. The groomer might want to spend more and more time alone with the child, drawing them away from their usual support networks and activities.

If a child challenges any of this behavior or starts to pull away, the groomer might use emotional blackmail or blame to regain control. They might say that their feelings are hurt or that the child doesn't appreciate all they've done for them, playing on the child's empathy and sense of responsibility.

Importantly, groomers often leverage technology to maintain control, using instant messaging, social media, and gaming platforms to create a constant presence in a child's life. This digital leash allows them to have uninterrupted access to the child, often without the parent's knowledge.

It's not uncommon for groomers to encourage children to take and share explicit images or engage in sexual conversations online. Once this content is shared, they may use it to blackmail the child into silence or continued compliance, a tactic known as 'sextortion'.

Being aware of these progressive stages and tactics is vital in preemptive protection. As much as groomers may wish to shroud their intentions in a veil of secrecy and companionship, knowledge and education are powerful tools for keeping that veil lifted.

It's essential parents, caregivers, and educators remain observant of changes in behavior or new adult interactions in a child's life. Equipping children with the understanding of appropriate boundaries, as discussed in earlier chapters, empowers them to recognize when someone may be crossing the line.

Please note, while these tactics are commonly used, each situation may differ. Not all kind or affectionate behavior from adults towards children is grooming. However, staying informed, maintaining open communication, and trusting one's instincts can help differentiate genuine kindness from potential grooming behavior.

Educating ourselves and our children about these tactics is a proactive step in safeguarding against manipulation. It builds a foundation of understanding that can help children feel confident in recognizing and reporting behaviors that make them uncomfortable. Remember, while the topic of grooming can be intimidating, facing it with knowledge and open dialogue is a bright beacon of prevention.

Section 3.2: Red Flags and Warning Signs

We've just explored grooming tactics and how they can be subtle and manipulative. Now, it's imperative to focus on the red flags and warning signs that may indicate a child is being groomed or is in an unsafe situation. Parents, caregivers, and educators, your watchful eyes and informed minds can make all the difference.

Firstly, let's consider changes in behavior. If a child starts to act differently, whether they become withdrawn or show outbursts of anger, it could be a signal that something is amiss. No change should be dismissed without consideration, especially if it seems out of character for them.

Another significant red flag is when a child receives gifts or money from an adult for no clear reason. These can be used as tools to build a secret relationship, one that thrives on secrecy and is shrouded in 'our little secret' scenarios.

Pay attention to a child's online activity as well. If they start to spend an increasing amount of time online, especially in private, inquire gently about what they're enjoying so much. This can be tricky terrain, but establishing open communication is key to understanding whom they may be interacting with.

Unexplained changes in mood or personality, such as showing signs of fear, anxiety, or sudden mood swings, should always be noted. A child under the stress of keeping a secret or dealing with inappropriate attention may exhibit these signs of emotional distress.

Isolation from friends and family can also be a warning sign. If a child becomes unusually private or starts to avoid social situations they once loved, it could mean they're under the influence of someone who's trying to control and manipulate them.

Overattentiveness or favoritism from an adult can be equally troubling. If an adult is giving a child excessive attention or treating them differently from others, it's important to observe and act on this gut feeling that something isn't quite right.

Communication with an adult about sexual topics or adult themes is an immediate red flag. No child should be placed in an adult's confidences about such matters, and this breach of boundary signals danger.

Secrecy is another aspect to be on high alert about. If a child starts keeping secrets or is being told to keep secrets from you or others, it's crucial to address this and reassure them that they can talk to you about anything.

Physical signs, too, cannot be ignored. Unexplained injuries, discomfort, or knowledge about sexual behavior that is not age-appropriate are deeply concerning signs that require immediate attention and action.

If a child seems to be avoiding a particular person without a clear reason or starts to show fear or discomfort around them, it might be more than just a simple dislike. Trust your instincts and the child's as well.

Changes in eating or sleeping habits, such as nightmares or bedwetting, can sometimes point to emotional distress or that something disturbing is happening in a child's life. These shifts can be reflective of bigger issues and shouldn't be overlooked.

Reluctance to go to certain places or to be left alone with someone is a particularly telling sign. Should a child express this, listen carefully, and explore their feelings without leading questions, but with a supportive and open attitude.

Finally, it's essential to recognize that if a child takes the brave step to share something worrying with you, it's vital to take them seriously. Children rarely fabricate such stories, and how adults respond can impact their willingness to speak up in the future.

In conclusion, reading these signs and understanding what they could indicate is the starting point for keeping children safe. We can't surround children with bubble wrap, but knowledge and vigilance can empower us to create an environment where children can grow up with the safety and security they deserve. Keep an eye out, trust your gut, and always take action when you suspect something isn't quite right. Our collective effort can be a powerful shield against those who would do harm.

Chapter 4:
Empowering Children to Say No

A s we transition from understanding the underhandedness of grooming behaviors, it's critical we pivot to empowering our children with the confidence to say no—a simple yet mighty syllable. Kids, just like little oak trees, are naturally resilient and capable of growing strong roots, but they need a bit of guidance to learn how to stand firm against unwelcome winds. The ability to assert themselves isn't just gifted; it's cultivated through practice, encouragement, and understanding the unquestionable right they have over their own bodies and choices. This isn't about defiance; it's about empowerment. Through nurturing conversations and thoughtful role-playing, we can solidify a child's conviction in safeguarding their own well-being without feeling guilty or rude. They learn to trust that inner voice that whispers or sometimes yells, "No," when something doesn't feel right. It's our role to embolden that voice, to let it sing out clear and unashamed, ensuring that when they need to use it—be it with peers, adults, or strangers—they can do so with confidence. Together, let's embolden our children to hold their 'no' with the same ease as they do their favorite toy, treasuring its potency as both shield and declaration. This chapter is all about that—transforming 'no' from a mere word into a powerful expression of self-autonomy and safety.

Section 4.1: The Power of "No"

Hey, let's chat about something small but mighty—yes, it's the word "No." It's sure packed with power, isn't it? Just two letters long, this little word is like a superhero's shield for personal safety and boundaries. When children understand the magic behind saying "No," they get to hold on to that shield and wield it whenever they need to protect themselves.

Sometimes, kids are taught to always listen to adults and be careful not to come across as rude, but wait a sec! That doesn't mean they can't assert their own feelings and comforts. "No" becomes especially important when a child senses something off or just downright wrong in any situation, whether it's an uncomfortable hug from an overzealous relative or a peer pressuring them into something fishy.

Getting to grips with "No" starts with recognizing that children have their own boundaries and rights. Yes, you heard that right. Even the youngest ones need to know their body belongs to them, and they get to call the shots on what feels okay and what doesn't.

Here's a thought for you: Imagine "No" as a bright, shining stop sign. It's what helps everyone pause and understand that a limit is being set. See, when children say "No," they're not being difficult; they're communicating. They're saying, "This is where my comfort zone ends."

But guess what? Understanding the power of "No" isn't just about speaking it; it's also about hearing it. It's vital to respect another person's "No," showing kids that when someone else sets their boundaries, it's just as important to back off and honor them.

Practice time! Yes, you can turn saying "No" into a regular practice. Just like a tree needs to bend to not break in the wind, role-playing helps children flex their "No" with confidence. They can say,

"I don't want to play that game," or "I don't want to eat that," and feel okay about expressing themselves.

There's strength in the calmness and certainty with which "No" can be delivered. Coaching a child to use a steady voice, to look someone in the eyes, and to stand firm all pack a punch behind that tiny word. It's empowering and tells the other person, "I mean what I say."

"No" also extends to group pressures. When friends coax them to do something they're jittery about, such as climbing too high or hiding a lie, "No" opens the gateway to follow their intuition and not just the herd.

Let's not forget the grown-up crew—you guys need to lead by example. When a child says "No" to something reasonable, like skipping brushing their teeth, there's space for guidance. However, when a "No" concerns their body autonomy or emotional well-being, it's essential for adults to listen and affirm their decision.

What happens though when someone doesn't listen to a child's "No"? That's when we boost the signal. Children should know it's okay to repeat themselves louder or get help from a trusted adult. That's using "No" to sound the alarm bells, and it helps keep them safe.

Remember, saying "No" is a life skill. It sails beyond childhood and anchors itself deep into adulthood—it's part of staying true to oneself, setting one's course, and not drifting with every tide.

All this talk about "No" isn't to say everything should be a no-go. It's about finding balance. Kids should feel just as comfortable saying "Yes" to the stuff they're excited and eager about, knowing they've got the power to make their own choices.

As tall as the mountains and as powerful as the seas, the word "No" stands out in the landscape of communication. When used wisely and kindly, it helps children navigate through life's twists and turns, keeping them mighty and bright, like the stars they are.

And there you have it—the ins and outs, ups and downs of saying "No." It gives children a sense of control and respect, making them feel heard and valued. Isn't that what we all want? For the wee ones to grow up into strong individuals who aren't afraid to speak up. So, let's keep encouraging them to embrace the full potential of that powerful word, for their sake and the world they're going to light up.

Section 4.2: Encouraging Assertiveness

After understanding the power that comes from saying "no," it's essential to nurture a child's ability to be assertive. Assertiveness is not about being aggressive or dominating; it's about expressing oneself confidently and standing up for one's own rights. This section dives into practical ways to encourage children to find their voice and use it when situations call for it.

Imagine being on a playground, where the rules of the game are unclear and sometimes, the bigger kids call the shots. It can be daunting, right? It's similar to how children navigate their own boundaries and the boundaries of others. Assertiveness training kicks in here, empowering kids to be clear and firm about their wants and needs.

First off, it's important to define assertiveness with children. Explain that it's okay to express their feelings and that they don't need to hide their discomfort or consent. It's standing tall, using a firm voice, and not backing down because their feelings are just as important as those of anyone else.

Role-playing is a fantastic way to allow children to practice assertiveness. It creates a safe environment where they can learn how to react in different scenarios. For example, you can act out a situation where someone is taking their toy without asking, and guide them on how to say "I'm using that right now, you can have a turn later" in a confident tone.

Positive reinforcement goes a long way. When children stand up for themselves, it's crucial to acknowledge and praise them. This boosts their confidence and reinforces that what they did was right. "I saw how you told your friend about how you felt when they took your pencil. That was very brave and articulate of you!"

Encouraging children to understand their emotions helps in assertive behavior. When they can label how they feel, they become better at communicating their emotions to others. If they're feeling angry or upset, show them it's okay to say "I feel frustrated when I am interrupted."

Teaching the difference between passive, aggressive, and assertive behavior is key. Use stories or illustrations to portray a child who doesn't speak up, one who reacts angrily, and one who calmly states their case. Discuss which approach is most effective and why.

Practicing empathy and active listening with your child encourages them to be respectful when being assertive. Explain that listening is as important as speaking and that understanding others will help them express themselves in a way that is heard and respected.

Setting up scenarios where assertiveness leads to a positive outcome can help children visualize the benefits of this behavior. Maybe there's a story you share about a child who politely but firmly declines something they don't want to do, and as a result, they feel proud and empowered.

Allowing kids to make decisions and have a say in everyday matters shows them that their opinion matters. Whether it's choosing a meal or picking out clothes for the day, small decisions build their confidence in speaking up.

Encourage children to negotiate and find compromise. Assertiveness isn't just about saying no, it's also about working toward a mutually beneficial solution. A child can assert their need for quiet time while offering to play with their sibling later.

Reinforce the idea that body language is a significant part of being assertive. Show them how standing up straight, making eye contact, and using clear speech can make their words more powerful.

Discuss the concept of personal space with kids. Just like how they have the right to their thoughts and feelings, they also have the right to their physical space. Assertiveness could mean expressing when they need more room or when they don't want to be touched.

It's essential that as caregivers and educators, we model assertiveness. Children learn a lot by observing. So when they see you speaking up for your needs in a positive and assertive way, it sends a clear message that it's both acceptable and effective.

And finally, remember to keep the communication lines open. Encourage kids to talk about times when they felt they were assertive and when they weren't. Discuss what they could do differently the next time. Praise their efforts and remind them that learning to be assertive is a journey and that with each step, they're becoming stronger and more confident in themselves.

In this journey of encouraging assertiveness, kids learn that their voice holds power, their feelings are valid, and their boundaries deserve respect. It's not just about safety; it's about nurturing a sense of self-worth that will carry them through all walks of life. By fostering assertiveness, we lay the groundwork for our children to become empowered individuals who can navigate the world with confidence.

Chapter 5:
Safe Use of Technology

As we've equipped our children with the power to say "no" and encouraged their assertiveness, we must now turn our compass towards navigating the vast and ever-changing digital landscape with the same vigilance. The internet, a world without borders, brings boundless opportunities for learning, creativity, and connection, but just as it expands their horizons, it also opens up avenues that require a watchful eye and a savvy mind. We're here to arm our little explorers with the tools they need for their online adventures, ensuring they can recognize the difference between a friend and a potential online trickster. It's about setting sail in the digital world while being anchored in safety: understanding privacy settings is just as crucial as knowing not to share personal information. Just like we teach kids to look both ways before crossing the street, we'll guide them on how to cross the digital road with care - showing them how to create strong passwords is akin to locking the front door of your home. With a balance of autonomy and guidance, we're fostering responsible digital citizens who can enjoy the wonders of technology without getting lost at sea.

Section 5.1: Internet Safety Basics

As we've gone over many fundamentals about personal safety and the importance of clear communication with our little ones, it's time we venture into the digital world. The internet is like a vast playground with lots of exciting things to do and see, but just like a real playground, we need to know the rules to stay safe online.

First things first, think of the internet like a big city. It has libraries where you can learn lots, shops where you can browse toys and treats, and ways to talk to friends and family, even if they're far away. However, there are also places within this city that aren't safe for kids, and there are people who might want to trick you into something that's not good for you. So, it's super important that you and your children know how to enjoy the fun parts of the internet city while steering clear of the risky parts.

Parents and caregivers, your role is akin to that of a guide. You're there to point out both the crosswalks and the caution signs. It helps to set up some ground rules about internet use. This could be as simple as which websites are okay to visit and limiting screen time so that it's just enough to have fun and learn, but not so much that it replaces other important activities, like playing outside or jotting down wonderful stories in a notebook.

For the savvy little netizens, always remember to keep your personal information private. This means not sharing your full name, address, school name, or even your pets' names with strangers online. These details are valuable pieces of your story and are not for just anyone's eyes or ears.

Creating strong passwords is like building a robust fort for your online information. Use a mix of letters, numbers, and special characters to make sure your secrets are locked away tight. And here's a pro tip: Don't use the same password everywhere, because if someone finds it out, they could sneak into all your online forts.

When it comes to friends, the internet can be a place to connect with people from all over the globe. That's pretty amazing, but it's also why it's so important to talk only to people you know in real life, like your classmates or family. Strangers asking to be friends online is a red flag and best to tell a trusted adult about it.

Did you know the internet remembers everything? That's why you should think twice before posting anything or messaging something you wouldn't want everyone to know about. Always pause and wonder, "Would I be okay with my grandma seeing this?" If not, it's best left unshared.

Parents, while children are navigating these digital streets, it's critical to stay involved—know what apps they're using and what games they're playing. Play alongside them sometimes. This not only helps you understand their online world but also builds trust and communication.

Bullying doesn't stop at the playground. It can follow you into your home through the internet. So, if you ever find someone being unkind to you, or if something makes you feel yucky or uncomfortable, it's not your fault, and you're not alone. Turn off the screen and talk to a grown-up you trust. They're like your personal superhero team, ready to help you out.

The internet can flash lots of ads and offers at you, but like a high-speed magic show, not everything is as it seems. Be cautious of 'free' offers or contests—they can be tricks to get your information or trick you into buying something. Always check with your grown-ups before clicking on anything uncertain.

Downloading stuff may seem fun, but only do it when you're sure it's safe. That new game or app might carry a hidden trickster in the form of a virus, which can mess up your device or steal information. Your guardians can help you understand which downloads are safe and which are not.

Chatting online is like using a walkie-talkie; you send messages back and forth. But remember, on the internet, not everyone is who they say they are. Keep your chats friendly, but never agree to meet up with someone you've only talked to on the internet. Those are plans that need a grown-up's OK—no exceptions.

Help your kids set healthy habits by keeping tech in shared spaces where you can peek over their shoulders from time to time. This also makes it easier to chat about what they're doing online, share a laugh over a silly video, or guide them away from something they shouldn't see.

Lastly, remind your little ones that the real world is as awesome as the digital one. It's essential to balance online activities with offline adventures. Encourage playdates in the park, arts and crafts, or family board games. These are the activities that create irreplaceable memories and real-life skills.

To sum it up, internet safety is about being SMART: Secure your information, Meet only real-world friends, Always tell grown-ups about strange online talks, Remember not to share personal stuff, and Think before you click. Keeping these principles in mind will help you navigate the online world with confidence and care.

That wraps up our basics of internet safety, but it's just the beginning. As we move on, we'll dive deeper into how we can monitor online interactions to ensure a secure and positive digital experience for our children, so stay with us as we continue on this journey of learning and discovery.

Section 5.2: Monitoring Online Interactions

As we swim deeper into the vast ocean of the internet, it becomes imperative for parents and caregivers to keep a watchful eye on the waters their children navigate. Monitoring online interactions isn't about prying into every detail but ensuring a safe and nurturing environment as children explore and connect in this digital age.

It's a balancing act, truly, one where fostering trust is as vital as setting up safeguards. When you teach a child to ride a bike, you'd keep a hand on the seat until they've mastered the balance. Think of monitoring their online interactions in much the same way. It's about guidance and support, not control.

First up, let's consider the platforms children are using. From social networks to gaming forums, every digital playground has its own set of rules and potential risks. It's crucial to understand these spaces, just as you'd familiarize yourself with a physical playground's equipment and corners.

Having regular, casual conversations about what your child does online can open up channels of communication. Chat with them about their favorite games and social media, show genuine interest. It's a way to be part of their online world without intrusion, and it sets the stage for openness if something unsettling pops up.

Remember, guidelines can't work without consistency. Establish and enforce clear rules about internet use. The amount of screen time, the types of content that are off-limits, what information should be kept private – these are all things that should be laid out and understood. Consistency creates structure, and structure provides security.

Setting up parental controls is another layer of precaution. It can filter out inappropriate content and protect your little ones from stumbling into the internet's more unsavory corners. Though they're not foolproof, they serve as a good starting point for keeping children's online experiences age-appropriate.

Co-viewing or co-playing can be fun, too. When you watch a video or play an online game together, you're not just bonding; you're also understanding the kind of content they're exposed to on a daily basis, which can further inform your protective measures.

Encourage your children to share their online experiences with you, and importantly, react calmly when they do. If they bring a problem to you, resist any immediate urge to restrict access completely – that can create secrecy rather than safety. Instead, use it as a teaching moment, discussing problem-solving and critical thinking skills.

It's critical to recognize the signs that may indicate your child is uncomfortable with an online interaction. Changes in behavior, secrecy, reluctance to discuss their online activities, or unexpected changes in device usage could all signal that something is wrong.

Keeping an eye on privacy settings can prevent personal information from being shared widely. Together, explore the account settings on each platform to ensure profile details are set to private and explain to them why it's important not to share personal information like their school, address or phone number online.

Model the behavior you want to see. Children are perceptive. When they see you being cautious and respectful online, they're more likely to mimic those actions. Lead by example by maintaining your digital footprint, and they'll likely follow suit.

Frame the conversation about online dangers in a way that empowers rather than scares. Make them the hero of their own story – one who wields knowledge as a shield. Teach them to protect their own boundaries and to respect those of others. Let them feel capable and in control of their online presence.

Consider having family agreements or contracts about internet use. This could include what sites are approved, what behaviors are expected, and consequences for breaking these agreements. When children are involved in creating these, they're more likely to adhere to them.

Get to know their friends, both offline and online. Just as you'd like to know who they're hanging out with after school, showing an interest in their online pals can give you insight into the social aspect of their internet use.

Finally, equip your little ones with the understanding that the online world — just like the real one — is filled with both beauty and potential hazards. It's all about navigating it with awareness and care. Monitoring their interactions is not about restricting their freedom, but rather ensuring they have a positive, constructive experience as they grow in this connected world.

With your guidance, they can learn to cherish the wonders of the internet while being smart, safe, and respectful digital citizens. And isn't that the goal? To prepare them to set sail within the digital expanse responsibly, having the wisdom and the tools to weather any storm.

Chapter 6:
Consent and Bodily Autonomy

In the vibrant garden of our lives, consent and bodily autonomy are like the roots that keep our personal boundaries firm and respected. Imagine your body as your own special house, where you are the boss, and you decide who can visit, and what kind of behavior is allowed inside. This chapter is your guide to understanding that everyone's body belongs to them and that we all have the right to say who can hug us, hold our hand, or enter our personal space. Think of 'yes' and 'no' as magic words that open and close doors to your house—and remember, it's completely okay to keep your doors closed if you don't feel like inviting anyone in. Let's learn to listen to the way we feel about our body and choices, because feeling safe and comfortable is always the most important thing!

Section 6.1: Teaching Consent Early

Understanding consent and bodily autonomy begins at a surprisingly young age. When we teach our children the importance of asking for and giving consent, we empower them with respect for themselves and others. It becomes the foundation for their interactions, helping them navigate the complexities of personal boundaries as they grow.

So, where do we start? Let's initiate the conversation around consent with simple, everyday actions. For instance, when we ask a toddler if we can give them a hug instead of just swooping in for the squeeze, we're showing that their personal space is valuable and should be respected. By modeling this behavior, we're setting a standard – let's respect each other's comfort levels, always.

Picture this: a family gathering with all the hugs and cheek pinches that little ones often endure. What better place to practice consent? We gently encourage children to voice their comfort or discomfort, reassuring them that it's perfectly fine to say "no thanks" to a hug or a kiss from Aunt Sue or Uncle Bob. And as parents and caregivers, it's our job to back them up and support their choices.

But what about sharing? Sharing is often hailed as a 'must-do' for youngsters. Yet we must teach kids that while sharing is kind, they're also allowed to have boundaries. If Timmy isn't ready to share his new toy yet, that's okay! We can explain to others that Timmy will share when he's ready. And that's consent in action – choosing when and with whom we share our stuff.

It's not just about what children do with their toys or whether they accept a cuddle; it's also about how they interact with other kids. Can they touch their friend's hair? Should they grab another child's arm to get their attention? Let's encourage asking first – empowering them to know that touching someone requires consent and teaching them to respect a "no" when they hear it.

As children enter school, the lessons of consent extend to how they play. Tag and other hands-on games are great fun but are also prime opportunities to reinforce the importance of hearing and heeding the word 'stop.' "If your friend says stop, it means they're no longer having fun, and it's time to pause," we tell them. When everyone's having fun, everyone wins.

Storytime can also be a powerful tool for teaching consent. As we delve into tales of heroes and adventures, we can highlight instances where characters ask for permission or respect someone's decision to opt out. These stories often become the framework that kids use to understand their world, reiterating the concept of consent in a context they love and grasp.

In classrooms or at home, role-playing can be especially effective. Kids can practice saying, "Can I play with that?" or "Is it okay if I join you?" These rehearsals prepare them for the real world where respecting others' boundaries is key. And when they see their friends or siblings participating, it reinforces the understanding that this is how we all should act.

A piece of the puzzle that's absolutely fundamental is teaching children that they have the right to their own body. We tell them, "Your body belongs to you, and you are in charge of it." This mantra stirs up the confidence to take ownership of their personal space and proclaim their boundaries loud and clear.

What about when touch is necessary, like at the doctor's office or during sports? We clarify, consent has its contexts. We explain why certain situations require certain actions, but we also teach children that they can always ask questions and should expect to understand what's happening to their bodies in any scenario.

Now, let's not forget, teaching about consent is not just a one-way street—it's a dialogue. We ask children how they feel about touches and boundaries, and we pay attention to their answers. This dialogue roots the idea that their feelings are important and should be taken seriously by everyone, including adults.

As kids grow and the world around them evolves, their understanding of consent will too. They'll encounter new situations – sleepovers, parties, and maybe even first crushes. Our ongoing guidance ensures that as they face these milestones, they're equipped with the knowledge that consent is universal and respecting it, non-negotiable.

We also touch on the difficult topic of peer pressure delicately. "Sometimes friends might try to convince you to do something you're not comfortable with," we explain, "but just remember, you can always say no, and that's okay." Reinforcing this even when it feels hard is another layer of understanding consent – the ability to stand firm in their decisions.

Lastly, as we lay the groundwork for consent, we also build pillars of empathy within our children. We teach them to imagine how others feel when their boundaries are not respected. "How would you feel if someone didn't listen when you said no?" we ask. Encouraging them to put themselves in someone else's shoes promotes a deep, empathic connection to the concept of consent.

In truth, consent is a golden thread we weave into the fabric of their upbringing. As caregivers, educators, and parents, we possess the power and responsibility to nurture informed, respectful, and empathetic individuals. By teaching consent early, we're not just setting them up for success in interpersonal relations; we're gifting them the keys to a society that honors and values every individual's autonomy.

Section 6.2: Respecting Choices and Feelings

In the world of learning about consent and bodily autonomy, we've just covered the basics of teaching consent early. Now, let's dive into an equally important aspect - respecting a child's choices and feelings. This isn't just about saying no; it's about honoring what someone else says, even when it's not what we want to hear. Kids, just like grown-ups, have feelings and choices that matter.

Imagine you're at the playground and someone else wants to use the swing you're on. You understand it's kind to take turns, but what if you're not done swinging yet? It's okay to say, "I'm still swinging, but I'll let you know when I'm finished." This simple example teaches children that their feelings and choices should be respected while encouraging them to extend the same courtesy to others.

Respect is a two-way street. If a friend doesn't want to share their toy, it can be disappointing, but it's their choice. This is a vital lesson in recognizing that we all have boundaries, and they're meant to be respected. Through experiences like this, kids learn that their feelings and decisions are valid, and they will start to understand why it's important to respect others' choices too.

But how do we teach kids to identify and communicate their feelings? It starts with helping them understand and label their emotions. Whether they're feeling happy, sad, angry, or excited, acknowledging these feelings is the first step towards expressing them. You could say things like, "It looks like you're feeling upset because you have to wait your turn. It's alright to feel that way."

What if another child doesn't respect their wishes? Teach your child that it's okay to seek help from a trusted adult. Emphasize that adults are there to help ensure everyone's choices and feelings are valued, creating a safe environment for everyone involved.

Through role-playing scenarios, kids can practice what to do when their boundaries are not respected. They can learn to assertively communicate their feelings. For instance, if a playmate is hugging them and they don't want to be hugged, they can practice saying, "I like you, but I don't want a hug right now."

It's also crucial to recognize that respecting choices and feelings applies to various situations. For example, kids should feel comfortable saying no to unwanted physical contact, no matter who it's from, and they should understand that others have the right to do the same.

What about the tough moments when kids don't show respect for others' choices and feelings? It's important to not shame or scold them too harshly. Instead, use these instances as teaching opportunities to discuss why it's important to treat others kindly and what they can do to make amends or improve next time.

Part of respecting choices also means celebrating when kids stand up for themselves and their friends. If a child tells a playmate, "Please stop. I don't want to play this rough," and the other child listens, that's a success worth acknowledging. It reflects their understanding of consent and respect for personal boundaries.

Respecting choices and feelings is not just about preventing negative scenarios; it's about fostering positive ones too. When children feel their choices and feelings are respected, they feel more secure, confident, and valued. They're more likely to extend the same respect to others, building a community of caring individuals.

It may sometimes seem like a complex concept for young minds, but it's quite straightforward when put into everyday contexts. By demonstrating respect for their choices and feelings in our daily interactions with kids, we model the behavior we hope to see in them.

Concluding this section, it's worth reflecting – as adults, are we consistently honoring our own and others' boundaries? Children learn as much from what they observe as from what they're taught. As caregivers and educators, it's our responsibility to act as role models, upholding the values of consent and mutual respect in all our interactions.

In the next sections, we will continue to explore how children can navigate public spaces safely and how we can collaborate with schools and organizations to maintain a culture of mutual respect and safety. But always remember, the key to respecting choices and feelings starts at home and in the heart; it's a lesson that lasts a lifetime, benefiting not just individual children, but society as a whole.

Chapter 7:
School and Community Safety

As we've equipped ourselves with the knowledge of personal safety and the tools to communicate effectively, it's time to extend that assurance into the wider world beyond our home's cozy walls. In the realm of school yards and community centers, kids should feel just as protected and empowered. Imagine a place where the hum of children's laughter mingles with the rustle of turning book pages, where every corner and corridor is a bastion of comfort and care. That's the atmosphere we're aiming to cultivate, right? With a little know-how and a heart brimming with courage, children can navigate these spaces with confidence. We're going to zigzag through bustling hallways and skip along busy sidewalks, all while keeping our safety compass pointing true north. Remember, every "hello" to a crossing guard and each "see you tomorrow" to a teacher stitches a larger safety net for our kids. So, let's take these next steps together, ensuring that every chalkboard lesson and playground game is steeped in security and smiles.

Section 7.1: Navigating Public Spaces

When talking about staying secure in bustling playgrounds, crowded malls or while crossing the street to school, there's a rainbow of strategies to remember, much like the colors of the crosswalk. Just as you look left and right before stepping off the curb, it's essential to keep your eyes open and mind alert in all public spaces.

Public spaces can be full of excitement and adventure, but they are also areas where children need to know how to protect themselves. The first step is recognizing that every place is different. Whether it's a noisy arcade or a serene park, each location demands unique awareness and safety skills. Children, with their boundless imagination and curiosity, should feel empowered to explore, but they must also understand the importance of staying close to a trusted adult.

In any public area, maintaining physical closeness to a caregiver provides a shield of security. This closeness should be a warm reminder, not a harsh restriction. Children should see it as a 'safety bubble' that moves with them - a bubble where inside it, they can still have a whole lot of fun and outside it, they need permission to step.

Speaking of permission, it's a magical word that dances around safety. Just as a king or queen of a castle decides who comes and goes, a child should know it's okay to decide who can enter their personal space. Sometimes, people may ask for high fives or offer handshakes. It's vital for children to remember that they have the royal right to say 'yes' or 'no.'

Now, imagine a treasure map with X marking the spot for the family rendezvous point. When venturing into public places like amusement parks or festivals, children should help choose and remember this special meeting place. This is not just any spot, but one that is easy to find and well-known, in case they get separated from their group.

Crossing paths with strangers is inevitable in public spaces. This isn't something to fear, but to manage with savvy street smarts. **Stranger safety** doesn't mean being afraid of everyone new; it means understanding that not everyone is a friend and that's perfectly fine. A polite nod or smile is enough, and there's no need for a conversation unless their trusted adult is there too.

Like superheroes attuned to their 'spidey senses,' children can develop their awareness. This means noticing things that are out of place or don't feel quite right. Trusting that gut feeling inside can lead them away from potential dangers and back to their guardians' sides.

Oftentimes, public events and spaces are loud and filled with distractions. Kids must learn to listen over the noise - listen for their names being called, listen to instructions from caregivers or authorities, and listen to their own internal voice that tells them how they feel about what's going on around them.

When it comes to personal items, children should treat them like a squirrel treats its nuts—keeping them safe and sound. This could mean a backpack, a toy, or even a ticket stub. Treasuring personal belongings teaches responsibility and ensures they have what they need throughout the day.

Alongside personal items, personal information is a golden gem that shouldn't be shared with just anyone. If a child is asked their name, where they live, or other personal details by someone they don't know well, they should find their trusted adult to handle the situation. This rule of thumb helps guard their privacy like a treasure chest locked tight.

With all these insights in their knowledge knapsack, kids aren't just taking a walk in the park; they're on a mission of mastery over their own safety. Encouraging them to be active participants in their security crafts a shield of confidence around them.

Everyone has a role to play. Parents, guardians, and educators can model safe behavior, like paying attention to surroundings and treating everyone with polite caution. Demonstrating these skills in everyday life makes it much more natural for children to adopt them.

Empowerment is the banner that children should carry, emblazoned with phrases like "I can keep myself safe," "I am aware of my surroundings," and "I know what to do if I'm lost." Echoing these positive affirmations reinforces the sense of self-assurance that comes with necessity, not with panic.

As chapters close and new ones open, life continues to be a wonderful mix of lessons and laughter. Exploring these public spaces is one of the countless joys of growing up, it builds precious memories and critical life skills. Keeping safety at the forefront, children can boldly and brilliantly paint their journey with every vibrant hue of wisdom and wonder.

So, while children skip through these public scenes, spinning stories, and soaking in sights, let them always remember the safety steps—like a compass guiding them through unknown territories. With these smart, yet simple practices, they become the captains of their own adventures, sailing through the waves of the world with confidence, courage, and care.

Section 7.2: Collaborating with Schools and Organizations

Building a safer world for our children does not just happen at home. It's a team effort that stretches into the hallways of their schools and the spaces of local organizations. Think of it this way: parents and guardians plant the seeds of safety at home, but it is the schools and organizations that help these seeds grow and bloom.

Recognizing that our children spend a significant portion of their day away from home, it's paramount that schools and community organizations are well-equipped to continue the conversation about personal safety, consent, and respect. We must work together to create an environment where children feel protected and empowered.

How do we start? First, open clear lines of communication with teachers, school counselors, and administrators. Understand the school's current policies and programs related to child safety and welfare. If you're not sure where to start, asking about the school's stance on anti-bullying, internet safety, and student's personal rights is a solid foundation.

After familiarizing yourself with the existing landscape, you can suggest enhancements or new initiatives. Perhaps they could introduce age-appropriate safety workshops, or invite experts to speak to students about personal boundaries and self-respect. Schools are hives of learning, after all, and learning about safety is as crucial as any academic subject.

Let's not forget about after-school clubs and sports teams. Many community organizations have direct influences on our kids. They should be bastions of trust and safety too. Make sure coaches, instructors, and leaders are trained to recognize and act upon any signs of grooming or boundary transgressions.

If a school or organization lacks a clear policy or seems indifferent, don't be disheartened. Change often starts with one concerned, dedicated person. Gather a group of like-minded parents, caretakers, and educators to develop a plan for introducing critical safety topics into the institution's culture.

Consider advocating for regular parent-teacher meetings dedicated to discussing children's safety outside the academic curriculum. These meetings allow parents to voice their concerns, stay informed, and build trust with those who look out for their children during the day.

Take the discussion online as well. Many schools and organizations have websites or social media profiles. Encouraging them to post tips, resources, and stories about personal safety could spread awareness and educate a broader community.

Remember to celebrate the victories, no matter how small they may seem. Every additional teacher trained in safety protocol, every new policy adopted, and every child who learns to articulate their boundaries is a step forward in the protection of our children.

Next, consider the importance of diversity and inclusivity in these safety programs. Children from different backgrounds might have unique needs and concerns when it comes to personal boundaries. It's important to ensure that the programs schools and organizations implement are sensitive to the nuances of culture, language, and disability, ensuring that no child is left behind in the conversation about safety.

Let's talk materials and presentations. Visual aids, storybooks, and interactive media are incredibly effective in conveying messages about safety to kids. Encourage your school to utilize these tools in their curriculum and make sure they're accessible, engaging, and age-appropriate. These resources can turn abstract concepts into relatable, understandable ideas for children.

What about the kids themselves? They can be empowered to take an active role too. Supporting initiatives such as peer mentoring programs, safety patrols, and student-led campaigns can give them a sense of ownership over their safety and that of their friends.

Collaborating with schools and organizations isn't just about face-to-face communication either. Encourage these entities to maintain a well-curated list of resources for further reading. They can host webinars and provide guidelines for kids' digital lives, as technology and the internet become increasingly integral to their daily experiences.

Let's not forget about the power of feedback. Encourage schools and organizations to set up anonymous reporting systems, suggestion boxes, or forums where both children and adults can voice their concerns or experiences regarding safety freely and without fear of judgment or repercussion.

In conclusion, remember: when it comes to the safety of our children, it is a shared responsibility. Schools and organizations are vital allies in this noble effort. Together, we can build a cooperative, informed community that prioritizes the well-being and personal security of each child. Their safety is our ultimate goal, and our shared mission.

Chapter 8:
Building a Trustworthy Support Network

As we pivot from the essential discussions on school and community safety, it becomes clear that kids can't walk this journey alone; they need a safety net—a circle of trust woven with reliability and care. Let's explore how to craft such a network, one that upholds the values and lessons from the chapters before. Picture this network like a sturdy treehouse, where the roots are deep and the structure is solid, offering a safe space for growth and support. This isn't just about finding 'safe adults' but also about nurturing connections with caregivers and educators who truly understand the significance of consent, privacy, and boundaries. These are the allies who'll reinforce your child's understanding of personal safety, echo their right to say 'no,' and embody the dialogues about respect and autonomy that you've initiated at home. Think of it as teaming up to form an invisible, protective shield around your child, one that guards against harm while fostering confidence, courage, and the wisdom to reach out when something doesn't feel right.

Section 8.1: Identifying Safe Adults

Now that we know how to navigate public spaces and the importance of respecting personal boundaries, let's talk about who you can turn to when you need help or just someone to talk to. Trustworthy adults are like stars in the night sky; they can guide you, light up your path, and help you feel safe. Let's explore how to spot these guiding stars in your life.

First off, a safe adult is someone who respects your boundaries and listens to you. They should make you feel comfortable, and you don't ever feel pressured to do something you don't want to do around them. Doesn't that sound like someone you'd want to have on your team?

Parents and guardians usually come to mind when we think of safe adults, and that's spot on! But what about when they're not around? It's smart to know other adults who you can trust. This could be another family member, like a loving grandparent, a caring aunt or uncle, or a trusted older cousin who's been known to be reliable.

Teachers and counselors at school also fill these shoes. They're there for you during the day, not only to teach you ABCs and 123s but to be there when you need a listening ear. They've got experience helping lots of children, and schools have rules to make sure they're doing their job right.

Doctors, nurses, and other healthcare providers can be safe adults too. They understand a lot about keeping you healthy and are trained on talking to kids. So, if you have a worry about your health or body, these pros are some of the best people to chat with.

But it's not just people with official titles we look to. Think about your neighbors or family friends that have known you for a long time. These familiar faces that have earned your family's trust over the years can also be considered safe adults.

Another safe adult could be the parent of a friend. You've hung out at their house, they've made you snacks, and they've probably helped you out a time or two. These are the kinds of adults who are likely to have your back.

Okay, so how do you know for sure if an adult is safe? Look for ones who have consistently shown they care. They are the adults who remember your birthday, cheer you on at your soccer games, and always ask about your day.

A safe adult also knows the rules about privacy and personal space. They don't ask you to keep secrets from your parents, and they never make you feel uncomfortable or confused with their words or actions.

Remember, safe adults should never ask you to do something that breaks the rules or makes you feel uneasy. If they are asking you to keep something secret that doesn't feel right, it's time to talk to another adult you trust.

Even with all this knowledge, it can sometimes be tricky to tell. Trust your instincts—if something doesn't feel right, it's okay to say no and find someone else to talk to.

Chatting with a safe adult doesn't have to be about big, serious stuff either. It can be about a problem with homework, a fight with a friend, or even just sharing something funny that happened during your day. The point is that they're there for the small things and the big things, and you never have to face anything alone.

And let's not forget about emergency situations. Remember those lessons about calling 911? Dispatchers and first responders like police officers, firefighters, and paramedics are trained to help kids in trouble, so they're definitely part of your safety net.

But sometimes, a safe adult might not be around when you need one. In those moments, it's important to remember other safety tips like screaming, running to a public place, or finding another adult.

Let's wrap up with this: Knowing who your safe adults are creates a circle of trust around you. They're your personal team of heroes, ready to support you whenever you need it. Keep their faces in your mind's eye, like snapshots in a photo album. They make your world a lot safer and a whole lot brighter, just by being in it.

So there you go, champions! You're becoming experts at identifying the grown-ups in your life who can stand with you and keep you secure. With this knowledge, the world's not just a playground—it's a place where you have the power to choose your own trusted allies.

Section 8.2: The Role of Caregivers and Educators

As we forge ahead, let's cast a heartfelt spotlight on the irreplaceable role caregivers and educators play in the lives of youngsters. These are the heroes without capes, standing on the front lines of a child's development, poised to teach, protect, and inspire. Their role is not just foundational; it's transformative in teaching children about personal safety, recognizing grooming scenarios, and understanding consent and body boundaries. They are the architects who help build the mindset and the defenses that children will carry with them as they grow.

Caregivers, the nurturing force behind every kiss on a scraped knee and every whispered tale at bedtime, carry the torch of safety from home to the outer world. They are often the first to mold a child's understanding of what feels comfortable and what doesn't. By being attentive and actively engaging with the child's concerns, caregivers lay the bricks of trust that set the stage for open dialogue about sensitive topics.

Educators, standing in their classrooms or on their virtual platforms, are beacons of knowledge. They introduce children to a world beyond their front doors. In teaching about boundaries and safety, educators have the unique ability to reinforce messages with diverse and inclusive perspectives. They can create a supportive environment where lessons about personal safety aren't just heard but are understood and respected.

Caregivers and educators join forces when they communicate consistently with each other. Through partnership, they can exchange critical observations that may signal a child's misunderstanding of personal safety or flag potential risks. They can also collaborate on educational materials, ensuring that the messages delivered are uniform and powerful.

One of the most empowering tools in the caregiver and educator toolbox is storytelling. Stories carry lessons across the threshold of a child's mind, gently and engagingly. Through tales that mirror real-life situations, complex concepts like consent become relatable and easier for little minds to grasp.

Practice makes perfect, as they say. Role-play activities, led by caregivers and educators, can empower children to act confidently in difficult situations. Whether it's saying no to unwanted physical touch or understanding the right to privacy, these rehearsals for life help children feel prepared and secure.

Celebrating each child's unique voice is another critical aspect. When caregivers and educators listen to children and value their opinions, it sends a powerful message: your voice matters. It's a confidence-building strategy that encourages children to speak up for themselves and others.

In the digital sphere, caregivers and educators act as pilots navigating the murky waters of the internet. By setting healthy limits, monitoring usage, and discussing online safety, they protect children from digital dangers while teaching them to be responsible netizens.

When it comes to recognizing grooming behaviors, caregivers and educators need a trained eye. Workshops, seminars, and continued education on the topic ensure that they stay ahead of the curve, equipped with the latest information to safeguard children effectively.

Consistent reinforcement of learning is key. It's not about having one talk; it's about weaving personal safety and boundary education into the daily fabric of life. Seemless incorporation of these lessons solidifies the concepts, making them everyday common sense for children.

The support network that caregivers and educators form around children can be as intricate and robust as a spider's web. This network doesn't just catch a child when they might fall; it holds them high, bolstering their journey through childhood with the safety and support every child deserves.

Anticipating the evolving needs of children as they grow is part of the proactive stance caregivers and educators must take. They foster an environment where children can adapt their learning as they enter new stages of development, ensuring ongoing relevance and comprehension of the lessons imparted.

Caregivers and educators are also guardians of respect for diversity. They teach the importance of respecting all kinds of boundaries— physical, emotional, and cultural. Understanding and appreciating the beautiful tapestry of the human experience starts with them.

Finally, when faced with the delicate situation of a child disclosing abuse, caregivers and educators are the first responders. Providing a safe, non-judgmental, and supportive environment can make all the difference in a child's healing process. Knowledge of the right steps to take is essential in these critical moments.

The work of caregivers and educators is never done, and the importance of their role cannot be overstated. As they continually learn and adapt to meet the needs of children, they do more than educate and protect. They empower the next generation with the courage to stand tall, the knowledge to stay safe, and the wisdom to thrive in a complex world.

In the next chapters, we'll continue to explore the vital topics of handling disclosure of abuse, nurturing healthy relationships, and fostering self-esteem, among others. But remember, all these efforts are rooted in the vigilance and dedication that caregivers and educators exhibit every day. They truly are the unsung heroes in the narrative of a child's safe passage through life's twists and turns.

Chapter 9:
Handling Disclosure of Abuse

In the wake of learning all about boundaries, communication, and the signs of unhealthy behavior, it's crucial to know how to respond if a child courageously discloses abuse. This chapter dives deep into the sensitive yet paramount course of action following such a revelation. Handling this moment with care and affirmation can be the turning point in a child's journey towards healing. It's about keeping your cool while your insides might be churning with shock or anger. It's about listening—truly listening—with an open heart and a steady presence that reassures the child they've done nothing wrong. Here, we'll explore how to acknowledge their bravery and create a space of trust and security, while also gently preparing to take the necessary steps to protect them and navigate the systems in place for reporting abuse. Remember, the way we handle this delicate situation can reinforce the child's sense of safety and trust in adults, which is pivotal to their overall well-being.

Section 9.1: Responding Supportively

As we touch upon the delicate topic of handling the disclosure of abuse, it's crucial that our approach mirrors a nurturing garden—a place where trust can blossom and resilience takes root. Picture a child, courageous and hesitant all at once, entrusting you with a secret that weighs heavy on their heart. How do we respond? Supportively, with all the love and assurance a child needs in such pivotal moments.

Belief is the backbone of support. When a child shares an experience of discomfort or abuse with you, the first and most vital response is to believe them. It's not easy for kids to open up about such intimate details. They're often scared they won't be taken seriously or that they might even be blamed. Start by letting them know that you hear them, you believe them, and most importantly, that it's not their fault. This reinforces the notion that they've done the right thing by coming forward.

Next, thank them for sharing with you. It might sound simple, but your gratitude shows the child that they did well in speaking up. It's a big deal to step into the light and reveal such private experiences. A 'thank you' can give them a sense of pride and validation for their bravery.

Maintain a calm and gentle demeanor. It might stir a storm within you, knowing a child has been harmed, but it's critical to keep a tranquil front. Children can easily pick up on our emotions; if we react with anger or shock, it might scare them or make them regret confiding in us. By staying calm, we create a safe space for them to express themselves without fearing our reaction.

Remember, our words carry immense power. Use language that is comforting and non-judgmental. Phrases like, "I'm here for you," or "You're not alone in this," can reinforce their decision to confide and help them feel understood.

Open-ended questions can be a gentle way to encourage children to disclose more about their feelings or the situation as they're comfortable. Steering away from why questions that may imply blame, we should focus on how, what, and who questions that allow the child to share without feeling pressured.

Assure them of confidentiality but be honest about limitations. Children need to understand that their disclosures may necessitate further action for their well-being. Explaining that we want to keep them safe and that might mean talking to other trusted adults helps prepare them for what's ahead.

Offer reassurance about what comes next. The unknown can be frightening for a child, especially after such a vulnerable admission. Explain the process in a way they can understand, ensuring them that their comfort and safety is the priority through each step.

Ask them what they need. Children may not always know how to articulate their needs, but asking signifies that their feelings and comfort matter. Validate their emotions and let them know it's okay to feel however they're feeling. This instills a sense of control during a time when they may feel very powerless.

Resist the urge to solve everything immediately. While taking action is necessary, sometimes kids need a moment to just be heard. There is a time for planning and responding, but initially, our role is to be a supportive listener.

Look after yourself, too. Hearing about a child's experience of abuse can be an emotional burden. Take time for self-care and consider seeking support for yourself so that you can continue to be a steady presence for the child in need.

Empower them by offering choices. Whether it's in deciding who else to tell or in small, unrelated decisions, allowing children to make choices can help rebuild their sense of autonomy, which abuse often erodes. Even small choices can affirm their right to have control over their own life and body.

Keep the lines of communication open. Let the child know that they can talk to you anytime, that this conversation isn't a one-time event. Their feelings might evolve, additional memories may surface, or they may simply need reassurance or more support as time goes on.

And finally, seek professional support. As caregivers or educators, we aren't expected to know all the answers but seeking guidance from professionals who specialize in child abuse can prove invaluable. This not only aids the child in healing but also ensures we're acting in their best interest every step of the way.

Children are our most precious treasures, and when they're faced with challenges that test their strength, how we respond can either fan the flames of trauma or help soothe and quench them. In 'Responding Supportively,' we don't just offer a lifeline in a moment of crisis; we build the foundation for a future where children feel heard, validated, and most importantly, safe.

Section 9.2: Next Steps and Reporting

After a child opens up about an uncomfortable experience or an instance of abuse, it's essential to know what actions to take next. Let's explore the steps for supporting the child, safeguarding their well-being, and ensuring the right authorities are contacted to address the situation appropriately.

First things first, take a deep breath. By telling you, the child has shown a tremendous amount of trust in your ability to help. Your response should be calm, composed, and supportive. Reassure the child that it was the right thing to do in speaking up and that you believe them.

Now, it's time to document what you've been told. Keep details as clear and as factual as possible without introducing your interpretations or feelings about the situation. This act will be crucial when reporting to the authorities, as it ensures that the child's voice is at the forefront.

The next move is to report the concern. Depending on where you are, the process may differ—you might need to contact child protection services, the police, or a school official if the incident is related to the school environment. Whoever the authority is, the key is to do it quickly and responsibly.

Reporting what happened can feel daunting, but remember, it's not about taking the situation into your own hands—it's about getting the child the professional support they need. When you make the call, be as precise as you can with the information you've gathered.

After that step, it's about maintaining stability and comfort for the child. Keep their routine as regular as possible while being emotionally available. Offer a listening ear, a comforting presence, and a visible support, but don't push for more details—leave that to the professionals.

Speaking of professionals, connect with support services that specialize in helping children after such disclosures. These might include therapists, counselors, or child advocates, all trained to handle these sensitive situations with care and expertise.

Remaining coordinated with other caregivers and institutions involved in the child's life is also paramount. School teachers, healthcare professionals, and other family members should be informed if necessary and appropriate, which ensures that the child receives comprehensive support across all domains of their daily life.

While confidentiality is key in these matters, be transparent with the child, in an age-appropriate manner, about the steps being taken. They should feel included and aware—not shrouded in secrecy which could lead to more anxiety or confusion.

As days go by, monitor the child's behavior and emotions. Changes can be subtle, so staying vigilant can help identify if additional support or interventions are needed. It's a difficult time, and every child will react differently—be patient and persistent in providing help.

Not to be overlooked is your own self-care during this challenging period. You can provide the best support when you are also taking care of yourself. Seek assistance or counseling if needed. Handling a disclosure of abuse is tough, and it's okay to acknowledge your need for support too.

Expect various reactions once the report is out. There might be investigations, legal discussions, or community reactions, especially if the situation involves someone well-known. Stand firm in the knowledge that protecting the child is of the utmost importance.

Furthermore, strengthen the child's sense of safety through empowerment. Continue teaching them about personal boundaries and consent, and involve them in activities that boost their self-esteem and resilience. This is a time for rebuilding, and each positive experience is a brick in that reconstruction.

Communicate with the child about their right to live without fear or harm. Let them know that no matter what happens next, they are not alone, they did nothing wrong, and they are loved. Such affirmations can be a balm during turbulent times.

Lastly, remember that this journey may not be quick. Healing takes time, and justice processes can be slow. Encourage patience and reinforce the message that no matter how long it takes, the goal is the child's well-being and safety above all else.

In wrapping up, it's vital to see reporting and the subsequent steps as parts of a significant process that underscores our collective responsibility to protect children. By taking informed and compassionate actions, we can become powerful allies in the fight against child abuse and the promotion of a safer world for all our little ones.

Chapter 10:
Healthy Relationships and Peer Pressure

As we sail further on our journey towards growing into confident and compassionate individuals, understanding the dynamics of healthy relationships becomes our compass. Picture this: you're with a group of friends, and everyone's ideas and choices seem to merge into one. It's easy to catch that wave and ride along, but hey, every star in the sky shines with its own light, and so do you! Navigating through the waters of friendship means learning about the give and take, the respect for "yes" and "no", and the power of being your true self. Sometimes, friends can act like the wind, pushing us towards uncharted territories. That's peer pressure, and it doesn't have to steer your ship. You can anchor down, firm in your values, and stand tall like a lighthouse, guiding your pals with the gentle glow of kindness and understanding. Embrace the rainbow of personalities that everyone has to offer, but don't forget to shine with your own colors. It's not about being swept away by the crowd; it's about dancing to the rhythm of your own drum, with friends who cheer for each beat you make.

Section 10.1: Friendship Boundaries

As we've explored throughout our journey together, understanding and respecting boundaries is a vital part of all relationships, including friendships. For children, friendships are one of the first places they learn how to interact with others outside their family. Let's take a stroll through what establishing friendship boundaries looks like and why they're so important.

In the world of booming laughter and shared secrets, friendships blossom. They often start with a common interest or a random act of kindness and grow into a bond that can bring joy, comfort, and support. But just like gardens need borders to flourish, friendships do too. Boundaries in friendships help children to understand where they begin and end in relation to others, aiding in the development of their identity and self-esteem.

What Are Friendship Boundaries?

Friendship boundaries are the invisible lines that define the limits and rules for how friends treat each other. They help protect personal space, feelings, and needs. These are learned through interactions, and each child may have different boundaries based on their comfort levels and personal experiences.

Why Are They Important?

Understanding these boundaries can safeguard kids from becoming overwhelmed, maintaining a balance of give-and-take in the relationship. It can also prevent potential hurt feelings or conflict by communicating clearly what is okay and what isn't. Just as a kite needs a breeze but too much wind can send it tumbling, friendships thrive with the right balance.

Personal Preferences and Comfort Zones

Every child is unique. Some love big bear hugs, while others may prefer a high-five. Some like to share their toys; others may need more time before they're ready to do so. Respecting these personal preferences is key to a healthy friendship, and it's essential that children understand that it's okay to voice their own likes and dislikes.

Setting Boundaries

Setting boundaries can feel awkward at first, but it's a vital skill. If a friend is being too bossy or demanding, it's alright to tell them how that makes you feel. If something doesn't feel right, it's more than okay to say no. Kids should know these aren't actions of unkindness but gestures of self-respect. Remember, a good friend will understand and respect your limits.

Recognizing Unhealthy Friendship Signs

There might be times when a friendship starts to feel uneasy. Perhaps a friend is asking you to do things that make you uncomfortable or is not respecting your belongings. These are signs that a friendship is tipping out of balance. It's important to recognize these early and address them.

True friends support each other, respect one another's boundaries, and can have different opinions or interests without it causing hurt. When kids understand that friendships don't have to be a mirror reflection, they learn to appreciate the uniqueness each person brings.

How to Communicate Boundaries

Communication is at the heart of setting boundaries. It's about being honest and kind with your thoughts and feelings. A simple "I'm not comfortable with that" or "I prefer not to share that right now" can be enough. It's a conversation that requires both talking and listening, and it's a skill that grows stronger with practice.

Respecting Others' Boundaries

Just as we set our boundaries, we must respect those set by others. When a friend voices their boundary, it's important to listen, acknowledge, and follow through with respecting it. This can build deeper trust and friendship, making sure everyone feels safe and valued.

Handling Boundary Violations

If a friend crosses a boundary, it can be uncomfortable. It's important to express this feeling respectfully and firmly. If a friend continues to cross the line, it might be necessary to take space from that friendship or seek advice from a trusted adult. Healthy friendships are based on mutual respect, and it's important to maintain this.

Learning Through Experiences

Setting and respecting friendship boundaries is a learning experience. Mistakes will happen, and that's okay. It's all part of growing up. With each experience, children can learn and adjust their own boundaries and how to better respect those of others.

The Role of Parents and Educators

Parents and educators play a crucial role in supporting children as they navigate friendship boundaries. They can provide guidance, model healthy relationships, and offer a listening ear for any concerns. By offering this support, children learn they're not alone in navigating the sometimes complex world of friendships.

Balancing Boundaries and Inclusivity

While boundaries are critical, it's also important to encourage kindness and inclusivity. Kids should be mindful to not use boundaries to exclude or hurt others intentionally. Inclusivity means making room for new friends and valuing what everyone has to offer.

Cultivating Empathy

At the crux of all this lies empathy, the ability to understand and share the feelings of another. By teaching children to consider others' feelings and perspectives, they develop a deeper connection with friends and learn to build relationships that are both respectful and enriching.

Friendship is a two-way street. Just as we seek respect for our boundaries, we must do the same for others. As children grow and learn, the knowledge they gain about friendship boundaries will not only protect them but also become the foundation of long-lasting, healthy relationships.

Section 10.2: Coping with Peer Influence

As we soar further into the landscape of friendships and peer interactions, it's essential to equip our young navigators with the compass of resilience. Peer influence is a substantial wind that can either guide our children to safe havens or steer them astray. Learning to cope with peer influence is akin to setting the sails for a steady and directed path through the exciting yet sometimes challenging seas of social interactions.

Let's begin by acknowledging that the desire to fit in and be accepted by our peers is a natural part of growing up. The playground, the classroom, and the neighborhood are all arenas where children encounter the pressures and influences of their peers. It's where they learn to assert themselves, negotiate, and make decisions that align with their values and safety.

To navigate peer influence effectively, children should understand the power of self-awareness. Knowing who they are, what they stand for, and the kind of friends they wish to have sets a foundational stone in their garden of interactions. It's about planting the seeds of confidence and watching them grow into a stance that says, "I am in charge of my choices."

Encouraging kids to talk about their friendships opens a window into their social world. This conversation allows parents and educators to delve into discussions around peer dynamics, addressing feelings of wanting to be part of a group, and also the courage it takes to stand alone when necessary.

The art of 'checking in' with oneself is a valuable tool for children. It involves taking a moment to listen to their gut feelings about a situation or a friend's suggestion. If something doesn't feel right, it likely isn't. Teaching them to honor these instincts is a crucial part of personal safety and boundary setting.

Role-modeling is a powerful teaching method. When kids see adults in their lives make choices that are reflective of their own values, even if it means going against the grain, they absorb this behavior. It shows them that it's not only okay to be different; it can be a source of strength and pride.

Developing a sense of empathy in children enriches their social toolkit. When they can put themselves in someone else's shoes, it becomes harder to bow to peer pressure that involves mocking or bullying another person. This strength of character can also inspire others to follow suit, creating a ripple effect of kindness.

Another strategy is to practice saying 'no' in a variety of ways. Not all peer pressure is outright and demanding; sometimes, it's subtle and persuasive. Children learn that 'no' can be assertive without being aggressive; it can be delivered with kindness but also firmness.

Of course, not all peer influence is negative; there are plenty of positive aspects to be celebrated. Friends can encourage each other to achieve goals, try new things, and be better versions of themselves. Recognizing and expressing gratitude for positive peer influence reiterates the joy in uplifting relationships.

In moments when children might falter, it's important to have a non-judgmental space to discuss their experiences. Mistakes are a part of learning, and knowing they have a supportive network makes the journey less intimidating. This support system encourages resilience, understanding that it's not about never falling but learning how to stand back up.

Building peer resistance isn't about creating a bubble around our children; it's about strengthening their ability to discern and navigate. It's giving them a telescope to see beyond the horizon of immediate gratification and peer conformity, towards a future where their choices align with their welfare and integrity.

Let's foster environments, both at home and school, that value individuality and encourage open discussions about peer pressure. Children should feel their opinions are worthy, and their decisions, no matter how different from their peers, are respected.

Games and role-play can be implemented as fun yet educational ways to practice coping with peer influence. Through these activities, children can experiment with different scenarios in a safe and controlled setting, preparing them for real-life situations.

Finally, empowering children to be leaders among peers rather than followers reinforces their sense of agency. It instills the belief that they can be the change-makers, the trendsetters, and the advocates for good choices within their circles.

As we set our sights on guiding our young ones through the terrain of peer influence, let's ensure the compass we provide is imbued with understanding, skills, and the courage to be uniquely themselves. In doing so, we create not just a map for navigating childhood friendships, but a blueprint for living authentic and fulfilling lives beyond these formative years.

Chapter 11:
Self-Esteem and Body Positivity

In the landscape of our lives, the way we view ourselves and our bodies plays a towering range of hills that can either uplift us to sunny peaks or drop us into shadowy valleys. Let's navigate this terrain together, fostering self-esteem and body positivity in our marvelous youngsters. Just like a well-nourished garden, kids' self-image needs regular attention and care. Hearths of warmth and love, let's assure our children that they shine brightly, just as stars of their own unique constellations in life's grand sky. Embracing every freckle, every curl, every inch of their being with joy, teaches them to bloom with confidence. We'll dive into this journey, not just skimming the surface, but really exploring the depths of what it means to hold one's head high with a smile that radiates from within. For when our children stand tall, anchored in the knowledge their bodies are their own respected temples, they're set to dance through life's adventures with self-assured grace and unwavering respect for themselves and others.

Section 11.1: Promoting Positive Self-Image

As we take this journey together, exploring how to impart vital knowledge to our children, we now arrive at a haven of self-discovery. The notion of self-image is central not just to how we see ourselves, but also to how we interact with the world and establish our boundaries. A positive self-image fuels confidence, and this confidence is our children's armor against many of life's challenges.

It starts at the core—with the seeds of self-perception we plant in the fertile minds of our youth. When a child looks in the mirror, what do they see? Do they understand the depth, the strength, and the marvel that stares back at them? It's important to help children recognize and celebrate their unique qualities, skills, and talents. Honoring their individuality encourages them to value themselves and others.

Acknowledging accomplishments can be a simple yet profound way to bolster a child's self-image. Whether it's a picture that's been diligently colored, a puzzle completed, or a new word learned, every step forward is a testament to their growing capabilities. It's not just about the big wins; it's about recognizing effort, resilience, and progress.

Compliments can be powerful—when they're focused on the right things. Instead of only praising outcomes or natural attributes, place an emphasis on effort, determination, and kindness. This nurtures an intrinsic appreciation of personal qualities that transcend the superficial and fosters a more sustainable form of self-esteem.

In a world saturated with media images of perfection, it's critical to discuss the reality behind these images with our children. With care, we can explain that pictures in magazines and online are often altered, and those fleeting seconds in ads are staged and curated—far from everyday moments. Helping them understand that real beauty is diverse and multifaceted can shield them from unrealistic expectations.

Encourage their endeavors, even those that end in a tangle of mistakes and missteps. Constructive feedback, wrapped in the warmth of your support, can guide them towards improvement without diminishing their sense of self-worth. It's about growing and learning, not just about triumphs.

Our conversations around body image and self-worth should be inclusive and empathetic. Children will have questions and insecurities—these moments are opportunities. Address them with honesty and compassion, ensuring the child understands they are cherished for who they are, not just what they look like.

Act as a mirror for the qualities that truly matter—their kindness, creativity, how they share and support their friends. These are the attributes to reflect back to them so they may see themselves through a lens of character and heart.

Storytelling can be an imaginative avenue to explore themes of self-worth and individuality. Share stories that feature a range of protagonists, celebrating different abilities, cultures, and backgrounds. Show them that heroes come in all forms and that they, too, hold the potential for greatness within.

When influences outside your home come calling, arm your child with questions. Teach them to critically examine messages about appearance and worth, asking "Who benefits from this message?" and "Does it respect the diversity of people in our world?" It's about nurturing media literacy alongside self-respect.

Involve children in activities that connect them to their bodies in positive ways—sports, dance, crafting, and more. It's not just about exercise for health, but movement for joy, expression, and the marvel of what their bodies can achieve.

Listen genuinely to their thoughts and feelings about themselves. Validate their emotions without immediately jumping to solutions or dismissals. Sometimes, the act of being heard is, in itself, a soothing balm for a troubled self-image.

Model positive self-talk and self-care habits. When children see their role models treating themselves with kindness and respect, they learn to mirror that behavior. Let them hear you celebrate your strengths and handle your own imperfections with grace.

Finally, remember that self-image is not a static picture but an evolving masterpiece. As days string into weeks and months, assure your child that growth is always possible, and they have the power to redefine themselves as they learn, develop, and experience life. Reinforce the idea that their potential is as limitless as the sky—always expanding, always full of new opportunities to shine.

As we conclude this section, let it be a reminder that instilling a positive self-image is both a gift and a responsibility. It is a foundation upon which children can build a life of well-being, resilience, and happiness. It's about more than just liking oneself—it's about recognizing one's inherent worth, celebrating it, and carrying it confidently into every avenue of life's grand journey.

Section 11.2: Body Boundaries and Respect

We've talked about the importance of nurturing self-esteem and fostering a positive self-image in the previous section. Now, it's time to delve into body boundaries and respect, which is another core component of helping our young ones grow into confident and safe individuals. Understanding and respecting body boundaries is vital for children's safety and well-being, and it sets the stage for healthy relationships throughout their lives.

Body boundaries are the invisible lines we draw around our bodies that define what is comfortable and what is not. Just like we have doors in our homes that we can close when we want privacy, our bodies have boundaries that we can set depending on how we feel. It's like having your own personal bubble that keeps you feeling safe and respected.

Teaching kids about body boundaries starts with simple concepts. It's like learning the rules of a game before you start playing. Knowing where the lines are helps everyone play fairly and have fun. And when it comes to body boundaries, it's no different. Children should feel empowered to express when they want to be hugged or kissed and when they don't, just as they can decide if they want to play tag or sit out.

Let's chat about how we can help kids listen to their own feelings about their body boundaries. One way is to encourage them to pay attention to 'uh-oh' feelings. These are the little alarms that go off inside when something doesn't feel right. It could be a tummy flutter or a pinch in their heart—whatever it is, it's their body's way of saying, 'Hey, I need some space,' or 'I'm not okay with this.'

Respecting others' boundaries is just as crucial as understanding our own. It's all about empathy, which is like putting yourself in someone else's shoes and imagining how they feel. When children learn to respect their friends' and family members' body boundaries, it helps everyone feel valued and cared for. It creates a circle of trust where everyone understands that 'no' means 'no', and 'stop' means 'stop'— no excuses, no exceptions.

We also need to talk to children about privacy and what may be considered private areas of their bodies. Emphasizing that these areas are special to them and that they have the right to keep them just for themselves is crucial. This is where the concept of 'bathing suit rules' can be useful, which simply suggests that the parts covered by a bathing suit are private.

Kids are naturally curious, and they'll have questions about their bodies and the bodies of others. Answering these questions with clear, honest, and age-appropriate responses will reinforce respect and understanding, and help kids navigate their curiosity without shame or embarrassment.

But let's remember, even the most well-taught child might face situations where they're unsure about their body boundaries being crossed. That's why we need to make sure they have a strong support system to turn to. Be it parents, teachers, or a trusted adult friend—a child should always know there are safe people they can talk to if they're feeling uncomfortable.

What about uncomfortable feelings children might encounter in public spaces or at social events where they're expected to give hugs or kisses to relatives? We should guide children in politeness and respect while also giving them alternatives, such as offering a high-five, a wave, or a cheerful 'hello' instead of unwanted physical contact.

Respect shouldn't be just a rule; it's a way of life. So, let's model respect and body boundaries ourselves. When we ask permission before giving a hug, when we respect a shy wave instead of insisting on a cuddle, we show our kids that their choices are valid and important.

Remember, reinforcing body boundaries isn't about instilling fear—it's about empowering kids with the knowledge to protect themselves and respect others. We're not creating walls; we're giving them the tools to build their own safe, flexible boundaries that can adapt as they grow and change.

In a world that's full of differences, teaching body boundaries can help children learn to cherish those differences and approach others with kindness and respect. Whether it's understanding personal space or the importance of consent, these lessons are the building blocks of every strong, caring community.

And let's not forget that each child is unique. What works for one may not work for another. It's like finding the right key for the right lock. Patience, persistence, and personalized guidance will help each child understand and embrace the concept of body boundaries at their own pace.

As we wrap up this section, think about how we can reinforce these values every day. It can be through stories, games that involve personal space, or simply praising a child when they express their comfort or discomfort about their body boundaries. It's about regular, gentle reminders that they are the bosses of their bodies and that their words have power and deserve respect.

So, let's champion body boundaries and respect, not just with words but through our actions, making sure each child feels heard, valued, and most importantly, respected. This isn't just a lesson for today, it's a foundation for a lifetime of respecting themselves and the people around them.

Chapter 12:
Continual Learning and Adaptation

As our journey through understanding and developing personal safety continues, we arrive at a pivotal concept—like the seasons, we must keep adapting and growing. The world doesn't stand still, and neither does the process of learning about consent, boundaries, and safety. Just as a young tree stretches its branches a bit further with each passing year, the conversations we have with our children must expand as they do. Nurturing their ability to adapt to new situations and refresh their understanding is vital. They're not the same kids they were last year, and the lessons we teach them shouldn't be either. Let's foster an environment where questions are welcomed, and knowledge is a living, breathing thing that evolves right alongside our children. With continual learning and adaptation as our compass, we guide them toward a future where they feel confident in themselves and navigate life's maze with the wisdom to stay safe, and the agility to dance through challenges with grace.

Section 12.1: Evolving Conversations with Age

Talking to your kids about safety, boundaries, and consent isn't a one-time chat. It's a series of conversations that evolve as your child grows. Just like a caterpillar transforms into a butterfly, your discussions will change as your child sprouts wings of understanding and newfound maturity. As you've equipped yourself with the fundamentals from the earlier chapters, let's explore how to keep these critical dialogues alive and growing through different ages and stages.

For the littlest ones, conversations are understandably basic. You might start with the concept of "your body belongs to you." For toddlers and preschoolers, this is reinforced through simple examples, like choosing which clothes they want to wear or allowing them to decline a hug if they're uncomfortable. These moments may seem small, but they're the seeds of consent and autonomy – and boy, do they grow.

As kids hopscotch into elementary school, the dialogues get more detailed. We talk about the different types of touches: those that are okay, those that help (like a doctor's check-up), and those that can be confusing or unsafe. Emphasizing the "check with me first" rule helps little thinkers understand that some decisions need a grownup's green light. It's a safety net as they venture into varied and vibrant social landscapes.

Middle childhood is often a blur of fresh experiences. Your child's world expands like a balloon ready to take flight. With new friends, activities, and autonomous steps, conversations shift to include online safety and the nuances of peer pressure. "It's okay to say no to a friend" is a refrain that helps them to carry their personal power into their peer group with confidence.

Pre-teens will find themselves at the doorstep of adolescence, where boundaries and relationships begin to take on new dimensions. Now is the time to talk about respect in friendships and crushes. Spark discussions about media messages and how they mold perceptions of relationships and bodies. Etch the idea that they are in charge of their own being – from the thoughts in their minds to the tips of their toes.

The twilight of childhood is adolescence, where kids are often storms of emotion and complexity. It's a dance of back-and-forth as they seek autonomy yet need guidance. Consent, in relation to dating and intimacy, needs clear communication here. Remind them that their feelings and comfort levels are the captains of their ship, especially in romantic seas.

Through each phase, the linchpin of these talks is trust. Reinforce that you're a safe harbor they can always turn to, even when topics feel awkward or heavy. When teens know they won't be judged or dismissed, they'll come to you – even when the waters are choppy.

Keeping up with their development means also updating your understanding. Let them see you as a learner too, engaging with resources or attending workshops. This models the value of continual growth and shows them that adapting to life's evolution is something even adults must do.

Remember to listen – truly listen. Give them the stage, respect their insights, and allow them to ask questions. Sometimes, they'll lead you to the next topic that needs unraveling. Their curiosities and concerns can be the compass for where your conversations should venture next.

Your approach to these lessons will flex as well. Kids can sense authenticity a mile away, so be genuine. If a topic feels tricky, it's okay to say so. Work through it together. In tandem, you'll navigate the complex roadmap of growing up.

Technology will increasingly be a forum for your child to express themselves, gather information, and interact with others. With the world at their fingertips, guide them on how to manage digital friendships and discussions around consent, privacy, and information sharing.

Finally, encourage reflection. As kids ponder over past conversations and situations, they mature in their understanding. Reflection is the polishing cloth that makes the lessons shine. Around the dinner table, on car rides, or even during a quiet evening, a simple, "What do you think about..." can ignite this process.

When the day comes that your child stands on the cusp of adulthood, these evolving conversations will have woven a protective tapestry around them, rich with wisdom, self-respect, and awareness. They'll step forward with confidence and the knowledge that they can always turn back to share triumphs, seek advice, or find solace in your support.

In conclusion, remember that the paths of personal safety, understanding consent, and recognizing grooming are not straight; they're labyrinthine, bursting with turns and junctions. Your guidance through the evolution of these conversations is the thread that helps your child navigate the maze and emerge empowered and enlightened.

Let this be your inspiration: with every age, you have the chance to layer new understandings, build new bridges of communication, and bolster the foundation you started. With patience, love, and a knack for listening, you'll help craft a resilient, aware individual ready to respect and protect themselves and others.

Section 12.2: Refreshing Knowledge and Strategies

Imagine a garden that thrives with vibrant blooms and strong roots. Much like nurturing a healthy garden, refreshing our understanding of safety, consent, and boundaries requires constant care and attention. In this section, we'll revisit some key ideas and strategies to keep these conversations growing strong and to help ensure they flourish among children, parents, and educators alike.

Let's remember that learning is not a linear journey; it spirals, allowing us to return to familiar topics with a deeper perspective each time. That's the beauty of refreshing our knowledge. Every now and then, it's important to touch base with the principles of personal safety and consent we've established with our children, to reinforce them, and to check how their understanding has evolved.

Think of it as a review session where the focus isn't on testing what our children know, but rather on reinforcing their confidence in the knowledge they hold. It's about making sure they feel equipped to use what they've learned in their everyday adventures. As kids grow, their worlds expand, and the scenarios they encounter become more complex. Our refreshers have to adapt accordingly.

Why not have a casual chat over dinner or during a car ride? Ask open-ended questions that invite your kids to share their thoughts and experiences. For example, you could ask, "Can you tell me about a time you felt proud for setting a boundary with someone?" This not only prompts them to recall what they've learned but also puts it into a real-world context.

Storytelling is another soothing and impactful way to discuss these topics. Bring out those cherished books that address personal safety in relatable scenarios and read them again. There might be details they'll pick up on this time that they didn't before. Stories allow children to imagine themselves in various situations and think about how they would respond.

Role-playing is a winner when it comes to strategy refreshers. It's a playful and engaging method that helps children apply their knowledge. Let's say you've previously taught them how to say "no" politely but firmly. Revisit this lesson by role-playing different scenarios, perhaps even swapping roles so they can experience being on the receiving end of a boundary being set.

As our mighty little learners venture into the digital realm, keeping them safe online remains essential. Build on the internet safety basics they've already mastered by discussing new apps or social platforms they may be using. Encourage them to think critically about the information they share and to recognize red flags in online interactions.

The delicate topic of disclosures should be revisited compassionately and calmly. Reinforce the message that they can come to you if they or someone they know is feeling unsafe. Highlight the importance of speaking up, and reassure them that their voice is powerful and will always be heard and respected.

The roots of self-esteem and body positivity run deep, and as children grow, so should their appreciation for themselves. Keep the conversation going by celebrating their individuality and encouraging them to be kind to themselves and others. Reinforce the idea that everyone has the right to feel comfortable in their own skin.

Importantly, as we refresh our knowledge, let's not forget to check in on ourselves as parents and educators. Are we practicing what we preach? Children learn a lot from observation. If we consistently model respect for personal boundaries and consent in our daily conduct, our little observers are likely to emulate that.

Now, does your family have a safety catchphrase or a code word? These can be fun and useful tools for communication. However, it's important to occasionally revisit their meanings, ensuring they remain effective and everyone remembers them. It's okay to update or change them if needed.

Knowledge evolves and so should our strategies. This means staying informed about new protective practices or resources that become available, such as apps designed to teach children about safety in an age-appropriate manner. Incorporating these into your family's routine can provide fresh ways to learn about and discuss safety.

Finally, while revisiting familiar topics, stay attuned to your child's reactions and feedback. The aim is to empower them, not to overwhelm them. Every conversation is a stepping stone building towards a future where they navigate the world with knowledge, courage, and respect—both for themselves and for others.

In conclusion, consider this refresh of strategies and knowledge as an ongoing commitment to protecting and empowering our children. Celebrate the small wins when they demonstrate they've internalized these lessons. Like the ebbs and flows of the sea, learning about personal safety and consent is a continuous process—one where we can joyfully swim alongside our children toward a future bright with understanding and respect.

Conclusion

As our journey through the pages draws to a close, let's pause to reflect on the key lessons and embrace the empowerment given to children, parents, caregivers, and educators regarding personal safety, recognizing potentially harmful situations, and understanding the vital importance of consent and body boundaries.

We've navigated the often-choppy waters of personal boundaries, understanding how to delineate and respect one's own space as well as that of others. Children now have a toolkit for communicating their comfort levels, and as caregivers, you are better equipped to support and honor these expressions.

Communication, we've learned, is much more than words; it's about fostering an environment where open dialogue flourishes. By role-playing various scenarios, kids can practice how to react in different situations, imprinting in their minds the confidence to act when needed.

Understanding grooming behaviors is like mastering a secret code that unlocks awareness. We've shone a light on these camouflaged dangers, enabling kids and adults alike to spot red flags and act preemptively to protect against those with unsavory intentions.

Empowerment echoed through our discussions as the simple yet mighty word "no" became a mantra for personal autonomy. Encouraging assertiveness isn't just about teaching kids to speak up; it's about cultivating the courage to stand strong in their convictions.

In the digital age, the safe use of technology is as important as learning to cross the street. From internet safety basics to closer monitoring of online interactions, we've provided the virtual road signs that herald both caution and educated navigation through the world wide web.

Consent and bodily autonomy are the cornerstones of self-respect and respect for others. Teaching consent from a tender age lays the foundation for healthy relationships and interactions that honor individual choices and feelings.

What about the space beyond the home? We explored the safe navigation of public spaces and learned how building bridges with schools and organizations enhances the communal shield that protects our youth.

We've stitched a safety net by identifying safe adults and understanding the multifaceted role of caregivers and educators in a child's life. It is the interweaved efforts of all trusted guardians that form the support network for our dear young ones.

When faced with the potential dark side of human interactions, handling the delicate matter of abuse disclosure, we've learned the importance of a supportive response, the necessary next steps, and the know-how for reporting to ensure child safety.

Peer interactions can be complex; thus, setting healthy relationship standards and coping strategies helps kids understand friendship boundaries and resist negative peer pressure. From playground politics to classroom camaraderie, children can sail through these social waters with integrity.

Lastly, fostering self-esteem and a positive body image are perhaps the greatest gifts imparted. When children learn to love and accept themselves, they inherently understand the essence of body boundaries and respect.

This book is not a final word but a living conversation that grows and evolves with your child. As young minds develop and mature, continual learning and adaptation of these concepts will cement a lifelong understanding and sensible vigilance.

In the spirit of never-ending growth, may you and the children in your care revisit these pages to refresh knowledge and reinvigorate strategies. With each read and each discussion, the lessons become deeper ingrained, creating a safer world, one conversation at a time.

As you move forward beyond the last page, remember you're not alone in this quest. A worldwide community of guardians and educators stands with you, all striving towards the shared goal of nurturing safer, more aware, and confident future generations. Go forth with the knowledge you've gained, the skills you've honed, and the conviction that together, we're building a world that treasures and protects the wellbeing of our most precious resource—our children.

Glossary of Terms

As we embark on this journey together, fostering a safe and nurturing environment for the children in our lives, we can't underestimate the power of understanding. Knowing the lingo plays a big part in bridging the gap between confusion and clarity. So, here's a list of terms that will help us speak the same language. Let's dive into the "Glossary of Terms," a handy resource to make our conversations and learning more meaningful.

Boundaries

Boundaries are like invisible lines we draw around ourselves to protect our bodies, feelings, and personal space. Everybody has them, and everyone's limits are different and should be respected.

Consent

Consent is a big word for an important idea. It means agreeing to something and saying "Yes!" with excitement and understanding. It's just as important to know that any "No" - whether it's loud or quiet - should be listened to and taken seriously.

Grooming

When we talk about **grooming**, we're not discussing haircuts or brushing pets. It is a tricky and nasty set of actions someone might use to try to befriend and influence a child (or sometimes, even an adult) to make them feel comfortable with inappropriate behaviors. It's sneaky and never the child's fault.

Personal Space

Personal Space refers to the area around us that we consider our private zone. Think of it as a bubble that keeps you comfy. When someone enters your bubble without your permission, it can feel uncomfortable.

Assertiveness

Being **assertive** means feeling brave enough to express your thoughts and feelings confidently and respectfully. It's like being a superhero of speaking up for yourself without being mean or hurting others.

Internet Safety

Internet Safety is all about knowing the dos and don'ts online to stay safe while having fun or learning. It's like a virtual seatbelt that keeps you secure on the information superhighway.

Autonomy

Autonomy is a fancy way of saying that you're the boss of your own body. It's about having the power to make choices about yourself without being pushed or pressured by anyone else.

Disclosure

A **disclosure** is when someone tells you something really private, especially about a time they may have been hurt or felt unsafe. It's a big step that takes lots of courage and trust.

Peer Pressure

Peer Pressure is when friends or classmates try to persuade each other to do something they might not want to do. It's not always about doing something bad, but it's important to listen to your own heart and head.

Self-Esteem

Self-Esteem is all about how much you appreciate and like yourself. It's like having a tiny cheerleader inside your head, always rooting for you!

Body Positivity

Body Positivity is a movement that's all about loving and accepting your body just as it is, and knowing you're amazing no matter what mirror or scale says.

With each term we've shared, you've got the tools to talk the talk and empower the little ones in your life to walk the walk, with pride and confidence. Remember, communication is a superpower, and with these terms up your sleeve, you're well on your way to creating a safer world for all our kiddos.

Appendix A:
Resources for Parents and Educators

We've covered a lot of ground together, and now it's time to provide you with the tools to continue this essential discussion beyond the pages of this book. The journey doesn't end here—it's a path you'll travel with the little ones in your care as they grow and navigate the world. Having the right resources can make all the difference in fostering a safe and informed environment for children.

Books and Reading Materials

The Right Touch: A Read-Aloud Story to Help Prevent Child Sexual Abuse - A gentle story that discusses the importance of private body parts and what to do if someone tries to touch them inappropriately.

Your Body Belongs to You - A simple book for young children explaining that their body is their own and they have the right to say who can touch it.

No Means No! - A picture book that empowers children to set boundaries about their body and personal space.

Educational Websites and Online Resources

Rainn.org - A comprehensive resource offering education, guidance, and support for survivors of sexual assault and their loved ones.

Kidsmartz.org - KidSmartz offers tools to teach children about safety and abduction prevention without invoking fear.

Childline.org.uk - Though UK-based, Childline offers a wealth of resources that can be beneficial for anyone looking to understand and teach about consent and personal safety.

Workshops and Training Programs

Stewards of Children® Training by Darkness to Light - This program provides adults with the tools to recognize and prevent child sexual abuse.

Positive Parenting Program (Triple P) - Triple P offers resources and workshops designed to help parents foster skills for safe and engaging growth.

Love Is Respect Workshops - These workshops aim to educate young people about healthy relationships and the importance of consent.

Remember that being proactive is key. Don't hesitate to reach out to local organizations that specialize in child safety, and take advantage of parent-teacher associations at your child's school to spread awareness and knowledge. By integrating these resources into your dialogue with children, you maintain a dynamic and supportive approach to their understanding of personal safety, grooming scenarios, consent, and body boundaries.

Each of these resources was chosen for their commitment to empowering children and the adults who care for them. They will provide you with a continuous stream of knowledge and strategies that can help kids navigate situations and feelings with confidence. So, pick up these books, visit these sites, and attend workshops whenever possible. The empowerment of your child starts with the informed support you offer every single day. Let's keep the conversation going and grow a safer, brighter future together.

Appendix B:
Activity Workbook for Children

Hey there, amazing young minds! Welcome to your very own super special Activity Workbook! We've been on a big adventure together learning about what makes you feel safe, understanding boundaries, and how to chat about the important stuff. Now it's time to put on your thinking caps and dive into some fun activities that help you remember all the cool things we've learned!

What Makes You Feel Safe?

Let's start off with a drawing activity. Grab your favorite crayons or markers, and draw a picture of all the things that make you feel super safe. It could be your cozy bed, a hug from someone you trust, or even playing with your pet. There's no right or wrong answer here; if it makes you feel secure, it belongs in your drawing!

Boundaries Brainstorm!

Up next, let's play a game called "Boundaries Brainstorm!" List down some examples of personal boundaries, like "having my own space" or "choosing who I give a high-five to." You can use pictures or write words – whatever you think is the best way to express your ideas.

Role-Playing Challenge

This could be the coolest part yet! With a pal or a family member, act out different situations where you might have to say "no" or ask someone else to respect your boundaries. Remember, it's super important to be clear and stand firm – but you can still be polite. Practice makes perfect, and soon it'll feel easy-peasy!

My Circle of Trust

In the Circle of Trust activity, draw a big circle and inside that circle, place the names or pictures of people you trust. These are the folks you can talk to about anything, like a trusted teacher, a family friend, or your super-cool aunt. Remember, trust is a big deal, and it's okay to be choosy about who goes inside your circle.

Online Safety Quest

Here's a treasure hunt for the digital world. Create a checklist of all the ways you can stay safe online, like not sharing your personal info, or only chatting with people you know in real life. See if you can do a little detective work and find out what "phishing" means, or what a "strong password" looks like. You're becoming an internet safety expert!

Friendship Map

Friendships are like a journey, full of ups and downs. Make your own Friendship Map by drawing two different paths on a piece of paper. One path shows what a healthy and respectful friendship looks like, and the other shows when things might feel not so great. Use this map to guide you in your relationships with friends!

The 'No-Go' Game

Okay, brave players, in The 'No-Go' Game, it's time to think about situations where you'd definitely want to say "no thank you" and walk away. It might be someone asking you to break the rules, or a stranger offering you something. Draw a big "X" on things you know aren't okay, and a bright happy star on the things that are safe and good. Trust your gut – if it feels wrong, it's a no-go!

Remember, kiddos, you're amazing just the way you are, and it's really important to keep yourself safe and sound. These activities are not just fun and games; they're your secret tools for being the best you can be. Keep learning, keep playing, and keep being the most awesome you!

And hey, if you ever have questions or feel confused, that's totally okay. Talk to a grown-up you trust, and they'll help you out. You're never alone on this journey. Stay bright, stay brilliant, and most of all, stay safe!